Don't Give Up the Ship

Also by Neil Steinberg

The Alphabet of Modern Annoyances
Complete and Utter Failure
If at All Possible, Involve a Cow

Don't Give Up the Ship

Finding My Father While

Lost at Sea

Neil Steinberg

BALLANTINE BOOKS

NEW YORK

A Ballantine Book
Published by The Ballantine Publishing Group

Copyright © 2002 by Neil Steinberg

Thanks to Leonard Nathan for permission to reprint "My Kind,"
originally published in *The New Yorker*.

www.ballantinebooks.com

Library of Congress Cataloging-in-Publication Data can be obtained
from the publisher upon request.

ISBN 0-345-43675-x

Text design by BTDnyc

Manufactured in the United States of America

First Edition: May 2002

10 9 8 7 6 5 4 3 2 1

For my mother

The sea does not reward those who are too anxious.

—ANNE MORROW LINDBERGH

CONTENTS

Contents

BOOK THREE

Homeward Bound

Don't Give Up
the Ship

BOOK ONE

Out to Sea

Being on a ship is being in a jail
with a chance of being drowned.

—SAMUEL JOHNSON

My father made me a boat. It wasn't a real boat, just the bed of a wheelbarrow, unscrewed from its frame, with a red plastic tub over-turned in the center as a seat. On a bright, hot summer day. We had a small wading pool in the backyard of our raw suburban tract and he set the craft in the center of the square of water. I might have been four. Excited and amazed at my good fortune, I climbed aboard the boat. And sat, carefully balancing on the unsteady vessel. There was a single moment of pleasure.

But my father hadn't considered the holes from the screws in the wheelbarrow bed. Four of them. The water jetted up, in gentle, dome-topped fountains, and within a few seconds the wheelbarrow boat sank to the bottom of the pool, which was less than a foot deep. I looked down at the water around my knees, then up at my father, who looked back at me.

This was not how the voyage was supposed to go.

Thirty-five Years Later

My father was writing his memoirs. At sixty-five, he felt the cool of the advancing shade and shuddered at the thought that what he held so dear—his years at sea—would eventually be lost. Every day he climbed the stairs to his studio, with a window facing the Rockies, and grasped at the briny ashes of his youth.

For a few hours his dead shipmates flashed and flickered on the pages in front of him. Scenes from nearly a half century earlier unspooled themselves. The characters moved clumsily, like puppets. My father struggled to make them real and alive, to smooth out the herky-jerky thrashing of their limbs.

But success eluded him. He saw the past, out of the corner of his eye, but could not look at it directly. He groped for but could not catch. Which was frustrating because he had been there. He was the same person. Wasn't he? A little older, that's all.

Okay. A whole lot older. And more tired. And more afraid, which is saying a lot because he had been very afraid, even then, as a young man aboard the ship, his great moment of fearlessness.

A minute passed. My father realized he was staring out the window at the snow-capped peaks of Estes Park. He unfroze, returned his gaze to the computer screen. He placed his hands on the keyboard. He tried again. He knew if he didn't do it, nobody would.

Well, almost nobody.

My father had been a physicist. Thirty years studying subatomic particles and weather patterns for NASA at its Lewis Research Center in Cleveland, Ohio. That may sound romantic and intellectual, and parts certainly were, but much was routine. He would set up an experiment, let it chug along for days and weeks almost without him, then study columns of numbers to make sense of what had happened or, more likely, what hadn't happened. It was like setting fifty mousetraps in a kitchen where you only vaguely suspect there might be a mouse.

He didn't stay in the laboratory long. As it does in many other fields, success in science floats you away from the part you love—the actual *doing* of the thing—until you find yourself a manager, worried about subordinates and funding and office crap. Thirty years, almost to the day, after he joined NASA he retired, at age fifty-seven. They gave him a commemorative scrapbook. He threw it away.

All that work, and science turned out to be unimportant to him. It sank under the ocean. The desire to memorialize life, which wells up so often in retirement, in my father's case did not touch at all upon the years of reactor cores and bubble chambers and proton targets that came after his voyages. Nor did it concentrate on his two decades of youth—the building of balsa-wood airplanes and radio receivers in the Bronx, that went before.

In the end, only the ocean mattered.

Just the four years—four summers, actually—between the time he was nineteen and the time he was twenty-three, between the end of youth and the beginning of adulthood, were what mattered. Were what whispered to my father, soft and tantalizing and elusive. What made him pause in the doorway of old age and try, try to turn back and take one last look.

Some evidence was clear. There were letters, for instance, and photographs, and movies shot on a wind-up Bolex. But the pictures only underscored the chasm between his life now and the person he had been then, the things that person did and why he did them.

It is a particular kind of hell to see yourself in a photograph taken when you were nineteen years old, handsome as sin, with jet-black hair and piercing eyes. In an officer's uniform—dress whites, they called them. Your ensign's cap tucked under your arm, its patent-leather brim gleaming in the sun. You, squinting at the camera confidently. On your way to Spain.

My father wanted to grab that young man by the shoulders, shake him, make him talk. How is it to uproot your life? To dare? To be turned down but to find a way? To win? To go to sea? What did that feel like?

A particular hell, to be sixty-five years old and see yourself frozen young in an old black-and-white photograph. Your whole life between you now, and the puzzling image of that handsome young man then. Your life spooling out like an impossibly long thread, one end of which you hold between your thumb and forefinger, tangible. A taut thread that you can feel and look at, yet a thread that goes off into space, and ends somewhere invisible. At the moon.

My father sat and typed at a small computer in his studio in Colorado, his paintings all around him, framed and hanging on the walls, or stacked against each other on the floor. Watercolors of wild waves and boiling seas. Rarely anything else in them—an occasional small wooden boat dwarfed by the mountainous ocean, mast broken, decks swamped, a moment from sinking. He worked at writing his memoir the way he does everything: intensely, obsessively, almost maniacally. He reviewed the pages again and again. He stopped painting entirely. He began calling former shipmates; most had been older than he and so were already dead.

Four, six, eight hours a day. Nothing else mattered. My mother complained that she was being ignored. She was lonely. But my father sat in his studio, his paints hardening in their tubes, and tried to write. He saw glory, saw vindication, waiting for him, just beyond his reach. He thrashed at it for a few weeks, a month, several months.

And then he called me.

I am a writer. Writing is the only work I have ever done. The last job I held that didn't involve words was being a baker for a Bob Evans Restaurant near Berea, Ohio. I was seventeen years old; one busy Sunday I baked 250 pounds of biscuits.

The routine drove me mildly crazy, even part time—after school and on weekends. Since I worked in the kitchen and never saw the public, I sometimes cut eyeholes and a notch for the bridge of my nose in the white paper headband of the chef's toque and wore it pulled over the top of my face like a mask. I would draw wings on the sides of the wide headband with a kitchen marker and slogans across the front. I once sang "Ninety-nine Bottles of Beer on the Wall" in its entirety, got to the end, called out "One more time!" and was in the midst of singing it again when the guy working the dish tank turned around, pointed the sprayer in my direction, and squeezed a burst of water. Eventually they fired me.

That's how it has been for me. I hate standing still. I can't concentrate for long periods of time. Everything I've ever written—articles, books, columns—has been done in twenty-minute bursts. Then I get up, get coffee, stretch, go do something else.

After Bob Evans, I went through nearly a dozen writing jobs: ad agencies, PR firms, corporate newsletters, suburban weeklies. Finally I slipped into a safe union berth at the *Chicago Sun-Times*, where I have been for thirteen years. I imagine I'll retire there.

All the while, I felt restless and empty, felt I was struggling toward some ineffable goal. Even after I got a column at the *Sun-Times*, three days a week, with my picture and everything, I couldn't shake off the feeling that this was the day job, the temporary mooring, until something real came along.

I struggled with the question—almost a philosophical problem—of whether my life seemed inadequate because I was chronically dissatisfied, a complainer, the sort of person who strides through the glittering gates of heaven, looks around, shrugs, and asks, "So this is it?"

Or was I dissatisfied with my life because it *was* inadequate?

The debate was a sham, an insincere show of open-mindedness. The fact was I knew the answer, in my gut. The hardwired conviction was there had to be more—somewhere else, somewhere I wasn't. Over my desk was displayed a framed poster from the New York School of Visual Arts. It showed a sign painter, sitting on a scaffolding and painting a big coffee cup on the wall of a building. Through a window next to his sign he sees an artist, standing before an easel, palette in hand. The sign painter leans back on his scaffolding and gazes at the artist. "To be Good is not enough," the slogan on the poster reads, "when you dream of being Great."

But even that is too genteel a spin on the feeling. This was nothing yearning or wistful. It felt like dying. When I didn't have a column at the newspaper, I used to say that not having the chance to write one was like being drowned, like someone pushing my head underwater and killing me. I was only a little surprised to find that having a column, three times a week, with my picture and everything, was also like being drowned. A few gasps of air when they gave it to me, the supposed moment of transformation. Then jerked back under the icy waves again.

* * *

News of my father's project reached me in Chicago like rumbling thunder, like word of an advancing storm. Over the telephone, he could barely conceal his glee. Something big was up. Something huge. He didn't tell me what it was. He wouldn't tell me. The implication was that I wouldn't take it well, this huge thing that was up.

I was used to this. I thought, *Good. Don't tell me.* It was only vaguely annoying. By age thirty-seven, I had steeled myself against my father and his interests. Long ago I had dismissed him as a person caught up in a lifelong thrall with himself—someone who, if I set myself on fire in front of him, would warm his hands over the flames for a good long time before suspecting something was wrong.

His excitement did not infect me. My curiosity was dulled by caution. I felt wary. I embraced the idea that I should not be told. I didn't want to know.

"That's good, Dad," I said. "You sound excited. I hope it works out."

Faced with my gambit, he dropped the pretense. Aw, okay, he'd tell me—dramatic pause—he was writing his memoirs. Writing about his thrilling adventures at sea aboard the training ship *Empire State*. Writing about being a radio operator in the Merchant Marine. Not only was he writing his memoirs, but he wanted—no, no, he was *willing*—to let me help him. As a professional writer, perhaps I'd be able to offer valuable critique.

My father was a friendless man. He had no buddies, no pals, he went for no beers after work with anybody, ever. Instead, he talked to me. I knew every atom of his life, particularly aboard the *Empire State*—or so I thought. Every tale had been drilled in so thoroughly that at times his youth seemed clearer to me—more real, more genuinely felt—than my own; and while I had certainly enjoyed the romance of the stories, over time I came to resent them, enormously.

I knew too much already, and anything I didn't know I was certain I didn't *want* to know. My father's life was like a decaying barn along-side the highway in winter. Something tracked in peripheral vision. A familiar sight, picturesque from afar, both mysterious and familiar. Half appealing, half scary, all the more poignant knowing that someday soon it will no longer be there. Yet nothing that I would ever pull the car over to investigate. The thought of stopping on the shoulder of the road, of getting out of the car, of standing for a moment by the side of the highway, trucks *blasting* by, taking a frosty breath, then crunching across the frozen farmland, to enter that gray barn, all darkness and cobwebs and hidden danger, was unimaginable.

We are a family who keep our distances. My parents live in Boulder. I live in Chicago. My older sister, Debbie, lives in Dallas, and for years my younger brother, Sam, lived in Tokyo. When people asked me why Tokyo, I'd say, only half jokingly, that it was as far away as he could get from my parents without leaving the earth's gravitational field.

But as the years clicked by, this distance, the existence of my family mostly over telephone lines, began to strike me as a mistake. I went to Japan and persuaded my brother to move to Chicago. And though I pressed my parents to do the same, to be near their sons and grand-children, they refused, blaming the weather in Chicago. I constantly protested, but in my heart I was glad—glad for the thousand miles be-tween us. A protective buffer. Once or twice a year someone would make the effort to visit. The visits were as inevitable as a Kabuki play: happy reunion leading to quick argument, genuine anger, false forgive-ness, real regret and sorrow, then parting.

"That's it!" I'd vow, slapping the steering wheel of the rental car, heading back to the airport. "We are never, *ever,* visiting them again." And my wife would smile and reply, "You say that every time."

So when my father phoned me at the newspaper during the middle of the day, as he always does, and told me about his memoir, I clucked vague, positive noises. But I also felt a shiver. This was a familiar pattern. My father, busily mining the subterranean chambers of his self, had discovered a fascinating new vein and was inviting me to help him dig.

Why should I? I was busy trying to goad my own career forward, flailing at it like a peasant frantically whipping an exhausted ox that has settled down into the mud to die. I look up, switch in hand, dirt and sweat in my eyes, and here comes my father, carrying a crooked staff, striding down the road, humming a tune, happily calling my name, volunteering not his help—Christ, not that—but mine.

I see you're not doing anything. Not anything important, anyway. Mind editing my memoirs?

Typical.

My father knew better than to press the issue in that first phone call. He was in no hurry. I would be updated in future calls. The work was going wonderfully; he had no idea writing was so effortless, so fun. The big thumb slowly pressed down. Maybe I would just take a peek at the memoir—for my own benefit, really. Maybe I could *learn* something. Over the telephone, I could hear him smiling. This memoir might be just the project I need, he suggested, to get myself out of my rut. To get going.

Months passed this way, my father lobbing his requests at me while I dodged and ducked. Finally he ran out of patience, or I ran out of wiggle room, and he needed a reply. So? *So?* I filled time. I hesitated. I stammered. I tap-danced. I had been given plenty of opportunity to prepare a response, but I hadn't found one.

My father hinted. He pressured. He dangled the possibility of shared royalties. Of his reflected glory warming my cheek. When these subtleties failed to ignite interest, he came out and asked me point blank to read the memoir.

Then I blurted it out: no.

No, Dad, I won't. Sorry. Go ask somebody else.

I refused, flat out, surprising myself and him. I refused because I had read his writing—his articles and speeches when he worked for NASA, and afterward the treatises and manifestos explaining and re-explaining his art. It was lousy in the way that only the writing of the educated can be: crafty, Byzantine, boring. Just to suggest how to fix it would take a lot of effort on my part and, lacking that detachment real writers need to improve their work, my father would resent my suggestions and fight against them. He had done so before.

I refused because I knew that, if I threw myself into the work, the day would come when I would look up and he would be on to something else. My father is a man of many interests, but only one at a time. He's always moving down the pike to the next fixation. If my attention wandered, at least it always returned to the matter at hand, eventually. My father instead touted whatever he had just read as vital for understanding the universe, pressing it upon you, before dropping his devotion for something new with an unfaithfulness that made me queasy. "Oh, the memoir?" he'd say, three months after I took the bait and began feverishly revising. "Are you still working on that? I've moved on to evolutionary psychology myself."

I refused because I was indeed in a slump and was afraid that reading his memoir would dishearten me further. The memoir's mediocrity would seem a reflection on myself, on my own skills. If my father could be deluded, could work so hard and produce something of such scant value, who was to say that I was any different?

I refused in honor of all the times I needed him and he wasn't there, because it was a nasty little joy to pull back at the moment he finally reached out to me.

I refused because I could. Refused because I wanted to. I refused. No, I said, no I won't, no.

"You didn't order me; you *asked* me," I said, during the endless rehashing that followed. "*Ask*. That implies a choice. So I'm saying 'No.' "

"If my father asked me to read something he wrote, I'd have read it," he said.

Your father . . . I thought, unable to juxtapose my dad with his own long-dead, cigar-chomping, sign-painting, joke-cracking, LaSalle-driving father.

Your father . . . if it were possible to hiss a thought, drag it through clenched teeth, I did so now.

Your father, I thought, *didn't tell you every goddamn thing that ever happened to him in his entire life.*

I said nothing.

There was a period of months when my refusal was politely ignored. My father continued to phone-in updates on his progress, as if I had expressed interest.

He passed on selections from the memoir to my brother Sam and sister Debbie—not his audience of choice but, as they say, any port in a storm. I congratulated myself; his attention shifting to my siblings meant that the problem would go away. Let them dance this one. But the memoir didn't go away. My refusal sat there and ticked. I was foolish to think it could be otherwise.

The issue erupted during my mid-winter Colorado pilgrimage, an annual ritual of building crackling fires in the fireplace, pouring big honking Manhattans, playing Scrabble with my mother, and listening to my father talk. He was still writing his memoir, still talking about it, talking, talking, talking about this book I wouldn't read. He showed me the letters he wrote to my publisher, behind my back, trying to spark interest in his work, proud, oblivious to their wrongness. I was as revolted as if he had been showing me pornography. I said nothing.

One morning in Boulder I was downstairs at the dining room table. He was rambling on about the memoir. I was drinking coffee, not listening, letting his words fill the air like static until he mentioned that the *Empire State* was still a training ship, still existed, after all these years— ry summer the *Empire State VI* still steamed crew of young cadets from the New York he ocean to Europe, just as it had forty-five sed that he was considering maybe, possibly, return-i , taking in a leg of the training cruise, just to feel the old r ks beneath his feet again.

my attention like a foghorn. The *Empire State*! I perked up tting up straight. "There's your book, Dad!" I said, slapping the table. "Nobody cares what you did forty-five years ago. Go back to the ship *now*. Have an adventure. Use it to frame your story. Go back and find out what made you care about it in the first place."

This shocked and, I think, frightened him. Having just said he was considering going back to the ship, now that I was urging him to actually do it, he backpedaled. I could tell what he was thinking: Going back to the ship would take . . . well, it would take effort. It would be difficult, inconvenient.

Certainly not as easy as padding up to the studio every morning to afflict the keyboard. Why work hard when you can just tilt your head and drain your genius into a bucket, then wait for somebody to come by and admire the results? That's what writing is, isn't it?

His inertia disappointed and disgusted me. So typical. The same I-was-going-to-take-you-to-the-circus-but-now-I'm-not crap I've been putting up with all my life.

I pressed him to do it, vindictively, because I knew he really never had any intention of going, or even to consider going, but was only pretending to contemplate the trip because it sounded good—that, and to hear himself talk.

"That's okay," he said, a favorite expression of his—words that are burned into my brain. Not in the usual, calming sense of "that's all right," but rather as a glozing, negating blow-off, a general forget-about-it phrase used to scuttle any project that strikes him as unnecessary.

I took another stab at plugging the go-back-to-the-ship idea. Emboldened by the realization that he would never do it, I felt safe to volunteer, maliciously, that I would even go with him, if need be, as moral support. We could go together. An adventure. Him and I. He and me. Father and son. Dad and lad. Pop and chop.

"That's okay," he said.

The visit devolved into our usual mess of rancor and bitterness. I couldn't get on the airplane fast enough. After I got back to Chicago, I didn't talk to my father for a long time. I flirted with the idea of never talking to him again. But that was fantasy; I knew the silence wouldn't last. I'm not that sort, though at times I wish I were.

His dismissal of my idea seemed proof that I had been right to ignore his memoir. I knew the past already. It was sealed, unalterable, like one of those little snow domes that I could let sit on the corner of my desk, or pick up and give a few shakes whenever I felt like seeing the snows of yesteryear. But it wasn't something I was going to explore. No way. I would never dream of cracking open the dome and trying to rearrange the little town inside.

And yet. I kept thinking about the ship. The *Empire State*. It was as if, having refused to read the memoirs, I instead began reconstructing them on my own. All the *Empire State* stories were so familiar. I had watched the home movies and viewed the slides—in that little dim chapel of memory formed in the living room by the gathered chairs and the white screen and the ca-chunking projector. I heard the famous tales a hundred times: the general quarters alarm, the dying captain, the distress flare at night. The ship sailed in my dreams.

His mementos from the *Empire State* were the curtains and wallpaper of my youth. As a child, I played with the ensign's shoulder boards from his uniform. I wore his radio operator's headset, with round black earpieces and thick cloth-covered cord, as the pilot of cardboard box airplanes soaring across the green sky of the yard. In the garage was the big reel-to-reel tape machine he used to record incoming messages and the black squawk box with its burlap speaker cover. They smelled of oil, of dust, of decaying rubber and deathless metal.

His den at home in Berea was filled with relics. A hand-tinted photo of the *Empire State* steaming into Venice, Italy. His framed radio operator's license. His chrome-plated Vibroplex telegraph key, with red Bakelite finger pads. An empty bottle of Spanish port, with a gorgeous, old-fashioned label that someone had signed in elaborate, feminine hand. His Turner microphone, a lovely piece of modern design, its head streamlined like an airplane engine nacelle, a crest like a Trojan helmet.

Thinking about the *Empire State* souvenirs, remembering how *present* they were, how revered—the bones of saints—I began to realize how important that time must have been to him. To him and, I suppose, myself. Growing up amid the detritus of his voyages gave me the impression they were romantic and exciting; in fact, they were the template for romance and excitement. Adventure was going somewhere, preferably out to sea.

My father, having been a radio operator aboard the *Empire State*, implanted within me a weakness for the old technologies. I expropriated the Turner microphone, for instance, and kept it on my desk for years, like sculpture. A symbol, not of my father, but of a vanished time, of technology as beauty, poignant beauty. A precious totem. A survivor of the shift. All those glowing tubes, quivering meters, dancing oscilloscopes—all gone, swept away by a few silicon chips. The progress most people my age celebrated and joyously embraced brought me a pang; I was an analog guy in a digital world.

My father later bought one nostalgic token to commemorate his adventure at sea. At about 100 pounds, however, it was quite a token—a Hammerlund Super Pro 600 shortwave radio. It sat in the den, next to his desk. The size of the freezer section of a refrigerator, the Hammer-lund was held in a special wooden rack my father constructed, de-signed so the radio would be tilted back at 45 degrees, like a woman tipping her face up, waiting to be kissed.

The Hammerlund had a lovely face. Gun-metal gray, with two big black dialing knobs, one clunkily stepping up the bands, the other spinning freely through the frequencies. Crystals, air vents, and all sorts of ancillary inputs and switches that were a boyish joy to snap back and forth. I remember my father opening the top—a heavy piece of metal that clanged shut like the hood of an old car—and pointing out the mirrored, industrial tubes designed to operate twenty-four hours a day, forever. I was impressed.

A radio like that needs an antenna. He strung a wire across the en-tire length of the roof of our nondescript suburban ranch house in Berea. It was supposed to be temporary, but it ended up being perma-nent, though he was always scouting around for something better. My father once called up a radio tower company and quizzed them so thoroughly that they fell under the impression he was placing an order. A misunderstanding that my father discovered one Saturday morning when a flatbed truck pulled into our quiet cul de sac with a hundred-foot tubular steel radio tower disassembled on the back. He sent it away.

I can't imagine what that tower would have done. With the antenna we had, we could pick up radio signals from China. Our household tuned to the British Broadcasting Company so often that we sub-scribed to "The Listener," the BBC's program guide.

As a boy I loved the Hammerlund. But I also found something ominous, almost frightening, about it, similar to the dark mystery be-hind telephones. The discordant bong of Big Ben introducing the BBC World Service news. The chilling tock-tock-tock of that sta-tion broadcasting the time from the atomic clock at the Bureau of Weights and Measures in Colorado, punctuated by that anonymous, official voice: "At the tone, the time will be nineteen hours, thirty-seven minutes, Coordinated Universal Time." Tock. Tock. Tock. Beeeeeeeeeeeeeep. Tock Tock Tock. "To adjust your equipment for sunspot activity, remember to . . ."

And the ships at sea. You could tune them in—that was the point of buying the radio. The Morse code spilling out an endless string of plangent whistlings. My father said that each had a pitch, a tone that you could identify—the dignified clickings of the *Ile de France*, the hollow cluckings of the S.S. *Rotterdam*, fussing like a Dutch hen.

I never caught the accents of the code. It all sounded frantic to me. The ships could have been trading the most mundane information about currents and headwinds, but the sounds struck me as urgent pleading, an endless wail for help. I must have needed that, as a teenager. I must have been scanning the horizon for distress signals and so tended to see them everywhere, in the same way that early nineteenth-century Europeans, themselves obsessed with the occult, discovered Egyptian hieroglyphics and decided they were ancient curses and magical keys to the universe when they actually were grain inventories and recipes for beer.

Once, late at night, I peeked into the den to see my father seated, holding a pad and a pencil. The radio was tuned to the ships at sea, and he sat at his drafting table, trying to transcribe the Morse code messages. But he couldn't do it. Twenty years had passed. He had lost the skill.

That memory of my father, in the den at night, mechanical pencil in hand, trying to transcribe Morse code, began to soften me. As harsh and condemning as I often am, it's not my regular state. I usually weaken, and slide toward reconciliation. The anger faded and I was left to assess anew. As if there had been a loud grating noise in my ear that, suddenly, stopped.

My own sons had something to do with it. I have two small sons. The younger, Kent, was a baby at the time. But the older, Ross, was about two and a half. Just old enough to begin showing a personality—which shocked me because the personality he began to show was mine.

There was no coaching. I did not, for instance, ever sit him down and teach him to fear the future. Yet there we were, together in front of the television, watching that season's dumb kiddie program. A show about professions—one tot wanted to be a veterinarian, another an airline pilot. Something like that. I sensed an opportunity.

"What do *you* want to be when you grow up?" I asked, with a parent's transparent slyness.

"I don't want to grow up," he said, plainly and with conviction. "I want to stay Rossie."

I mumbled something about how he'd always be Rossie, even when he grew up—the standard line. But I was amazed and troubled. It was no fluke statement. He didn't want to go to school either, didn't want anything to change, ever. He was becoming exactly as I was. Even as a little boy, I was nostalgic and timid. Not keen to meet the world, preferring to stay behind. I made my mother pull me out of nursery school. I had a good home. Why leave? My father's deep veneration for the sea had never inspired me to consider doing something similar—not once, not for a single moment—until that morning in Colorado. I had been so quick to condemn him, in my mind, for not wanting to go back. But at least he went, initially. What had I done comparable? Nothing. College, a miscue job in Los Angeles, then—*boom!*—a lifetime of hack journalism in Chicago. Maybe that's why I was so resistant to my father's memoirs. Just jealous. No women of Spain for me.

One evening the boys were taking a bath. I stepped out of the room to get towels, and in my absence they mischievously threw their bath toys out of the tub. They have a lot of bath toys. When I returned, the boys were so proud, so sparkly and beaming and wet, that I wasn't even angry. Kneeling to slowly pick up the toys, I wondered, When do they become fearful and sad? And will I do that to them? Or will the world? Or some tacit conspiracy between the two?

No question Ross was becoming the person I am—or some version of that person—whether I liked it or not. And Kent would follow. But was that good? It all depended, I realized, on who I was—whether I was a happy person, a good person, a strong person, the sort of person I'd want my kids to be. As I wrestled with that eternal question, it dawned on me that I am my father, in a somewhat altered form: I have my own fixations, my own bottomless ability to be pedantic and fearful and a bore. Before I inflicted my full personality blindly upon my sons, the way my father did, the way fathers generally do, perhaps it would be a noble gesture to at least try to understand who I am. And the best way to do that, of course, would be to understand who my father was. Who my father is.

Sure, I thought I knew him already. But isn't that the bedrock of error: confidence? Misplaced confidence? The issue would not go away. I began to feel certain of that. Even if I refused to read the memoir, one day it would return. One day I'd find it, a pathetic sheaf in the bottom of a drawer in a desk I'd be cleaning out after he was dead. I'd read it then. How could I not? I'd read it then, one day, sitting alone in that big studio, cardboard boxes all around. I'd read it as just another amateur's stillborn monstrosity kept in a jar. Each fractured sentence would be an indictment, each cliché a finger pointing at me. It would crush my heart. One day.

Too late then. But not too late now. So I considered it anew, and realized that I had been insincere, a few months earlier in Colorado, when I offered to go back with him on the ship. I had offered knowing he would not accept. That wasn't an offer at all. The key is not to offer, but to insist. That's how I got Sam back from Japan—not by asking him, but by telling him: You live in hell there; your apartment is smaller than my bathroom; the people there hate you on sight; come home to Chicago. And he did. Equivocation is fatal to persuasion. The ship had to become essential, had to be an undeniable quest. I would read the memoir and we would go on the ship, together. Period. The two would be tied. Who knows? Maybe there was something overlooked, something left to say. Maybe, in the close quarters of a ship at sea, we would find a way to say it. Maybe the ship *was* essential. Anyway, we would go and find out.

That may be rationalization after the fact. The core truth is that the memoir was an unexpected breach in my father's wall. A weakness. Sure, it was all about him, again, but he needed me in this instance. He couldn't write and I could. Maybe he did indeed turn to me because I was the only writer he knew. But I would accept, not because I was a writer but because I was his son. It was emotional judo, using his own momentum against him.

Anyway, I abruptly hurled myself into the breach, the way a man whistling down the street suddenly pitches himself over a bridge railing. Shoulders back, spine straight, a wide grin of embarrassment stuck on my face, I placed the call. "Dad?" I said. "Dad, you know that memoir? Could you send it to me? I've decided to look at it, after all, before we go on the ship." We were rolling seaward.

CHAPTER 1

The Sea Stumbles
— The Bronx, 1999

The big morning finally arrived. My father and I did our sweeping checks of the room, the V.I.P. Suite at the State University of New York's Maritime College in the Bronx. Thin industrial carpeting over a concrete floor, nautical prints, spartan and sturdy furniture; a state college's idea of luxury. We peered under beds, searched every drawer and closet, even those we had never used, not wanting to leave anything behind, trying to be smart and thorough.

We wheeled our suitcases into the bright 7 A.M. mid-May sunshine and across the Maritime campus. Mostly 1950s brick buildings, square and charmless, set in the shadow of the Throgs Neck Bridge, but also Fort Schuyler, an 1830s pentagonal stone structure built to defend Hell Gate against the British, with thick walls and gun slits and a parade ground. We walked toward the *Empire State*—our ship for the next month, sailing down the coast to the Caribbean and then across the Atlantic to Italy—gleaming white at the pier. The *Empire State VI* began her life as a freighter and, from a distance, had no ele-

gant line, no graceful sweep. She seemed cobbled-together, a long expanse of bow in front topped with an elaborate nest of booms and
cranes, a pair of lifeboats just ahead of the superstructure, then a clut-
ter of decks. At the stern, a large shipping container and what looked
like a pair of small orange submarines. The single smokestack was
stubby, practical, yellowish beige, with the SUNY seal on it.

The pier was hectic with a festive, summer-camp sort of commotion, busy with families, girlfriends, boyfriends, and cadets—trim teens
in bright white shirts and dark navy pants, their "salt-and-pepper" uniforms. They towered over their parents. Mothers held bunches of balloons. Fathers lugged big portable coolers, cases of soda, cases of juice.
I worried that we were unprepared—we had no juice—and puzzled
over the balloons. At least a dozen families had brought bunches of
them. They seemed an odd, child's birthday party touch.

My father stopped short and I ran thud into him, like a vaudeville
act. Disentangling ourselves and our rolling luggage, I wondered, *Is
this how it's going to be? Frick and Frack?* I looked around to see if anybody had noticed.

Turning onto Dock 19, where the ship was tied up, I saw that the
pier was named for A. F. Olivet, the no-nonsense captain during my father's cruises. I paused to make note of that, and of the dinghies
moored under a protective wooden roof leading to the ship. They had
bold, forward-straining names: *Courageous, Freedom, America, Magic.*

Looking up, I saw that my father, the good New Yorker, had kept
walking. I called to him—"Dad! Wait!"—and he turned. "I'll go
slow," he shouted back. But he didn't go slow. He strode toward the
ship. I hurried after him, the luggage wheels humming against the
concrete.

I got alongside the ship, almost to the gangway, just in time to see
him go up without me, lugging his suitcase, a wide smile spread across
his face. He said something pleasant to the officer at the top of the
gangway and disappeared inside the *Empire State.* I stood on the pier a

moment, shocked, then raced after him, hefting my suitcase in both hands and clattering up the awkward low metal steps. After months of arranging—the conversations, the phone calls, the formal letters, the visits—I had figured that our boarding the ship would be an obvious moment of high drama: an exchange of loving glances, a pat on the back, a shy filial smile, a fatherly ruffle of the hair, a deep breath and up we go together, arms linked. Ta-daaaaaaaah!

Not in this life.

"What's your hurry, *sailor*?" I hissed, out of breath, catching up to him at the cabin, C1, marked by a note card reading MR. STIEN-BURG SR. and MR. STIENBURG JR.

He offered this explanation: he wanted to get his suitcase aboard before the tide came in, raising the angle of the gangway, making it more difficult to walk up. He actually said this. Stunned, I turned away, puzzling whether his excuse was a mountainous lie or, worse, a sincere delusion.

I stood in the bathroom and looked at myself in the mirror: how was I going to do this? Six weeks with my father. A month at sea, then ten days in Italy. We'd kill each other. Or I'd kill him. Or myself. Or *he'd* kill me. One way or another, somebody was going to be killed.

Then the anger, a hot fluid at the back of my brain, drained away and I almost laughed—the *tide*, so ridiculous—and I remembered that, up to this moment, I had been genuinely worried my father wouldn't get on the ship at all. That despite his promises, when the moment finally came, he would freeze up on the gangway. Many times I had imagined, not entirely without pleasure, him grasping the handrails, white knuckled, rigid, me behind him, ramming the heel of my hand into the small of his back, forcing him forward. *"Get on the goddamn ship, Dad!"*

That had been the preconception. The reality was 180 degrees opposite. Instead of hanging back, fearful, needing a shove, he had raced ahead, excited, forgetting all about me. Realizing this shocked away the anger. It struck me that, after all these years, I didn't know my father at all. Not a bit.

We stowed our luggage in the cabin. When we had seen it for the first time, the night before, it had seemed huge, but now it looked very small. Two single beds, bolted to the floor, nineteen inches apart. Between them, a single square window, facing forward, offering the vista of the foredeck, the length of a football field but half as wide. The window couldn't open. Across from the window, a combination desk/dresser/counter, with a big mirror filling the wall above. One plastic desk chair and one padded chair, just fitting between the desk and the door. The walls were metal, painted an industrial green.

Remembering my father's stories of his first roommate dictating who went where, I hung back and let him pick his bed and closet. Respect. He took bed number 1 and closet number 1. I took bed and closet number 2. That seemed fitting.

I set my laptop computer on the desk. The newspaper had refused to grant me the leave I requested. Instead, they insisted I file my column from the sea. Still, given how I had botched my request, I was relieved they let me go at all.

Newspaper editors-in-chief are not famous for their bonhomie, and my boss at the *Sun-Times*, Nigel Wade, was perhaps more aloof than most. A large, ruddy, well-tailored New Zealander with a dramatic head of silvery hair, he was not given to long, friendly exchanges with the staff. Or even short friendly exchanges.

Granted, it would have been difficult to pick a worse moment to bring up the trip. I had written a column about not having an idea for a column—something I thought was very hip, very Seinfeld, and also happened to be true, always a plus in journalism. I enjoyed puncturing the notion of columnist-as-infallible-font-of-endless-wisdom and admired the portrait I painted of myself slumped before the computer, mouth open, head empty. "This must be what stupid people feel like all the time," I wrote.

Nigel hated it. "If you can't think of an idea for your *coh*-lum, then perhaps you should not be writing a *coh*-lum," he said, after I was summoned to his office for a chewing out. At first I bristled—the column *did* have an idea behind it: not having an idea for a column. He just didn't like my argument, didn't like the suggestion that some days there is no insight to sell for 35 cents. That didn't go over well, either. I tried a second approach: I was tired, working very hard, maybe the grind was getting to me, but I certainly still had something left to say. He liked that better. I was off the hook. The flames died down and we entered in that phase of relaxation that comes after a tense talk— the raking of embers, decompressing back into the workday, when I unwisely said something along the lines of, "Besides, I've got this ocean voyage with my dad coming up and will need to take off a few months from work; that should give me a chance to recharge my batteries."

What could I have been expecting? "A nautical adventure? Jolly good! Splendid. Just the medicine for you. Don't know why you waste your time on all this *newspaper* nonsense, anyway. We must lift a few brandies at the 410 Club before you sail."

The actuality was different.

"Fuck off, then!" Nigel shouted, leaping up and waving me toward the door. "Fuck off! Get out of here! Go work for a newspaper that'll put up with that *shit*!" I fled, backing out of the office, babbling apologies, hands spread in defensive entreaty, almost bowing. Not the heigh-ho send-off I might have hoped for.

Just before the *Empire State* sailed, my father and I went back down to the pier, to walk around on land one last time, more relaxed, without the physical and psychological burden of our luggage. People were hugging. A girl sat on the low concrete wall by the water and wept. Their own stories being forged, I thought. Would their unborn children someday be drawn to sea after them, sucked into the vortex of their parents' romantic notions? I sent a mental message of solidarity to those unborn voyagers: good luck, kiddos, I'm with you!

Departure approached and we went back aboard, together. Officials from the college, alumni, all sorts of people crowded the officers' lounge on the cabin deck and along the rails outside, picking at cheese and pretzels—a cocktail party without the cocktails. The school's public relations man, Stan Melasky, showed us off: the newspaper columnist and his father, returning to his former ship, where Steinberg *père* had been a radio operator in the early 1950s. Dignitaries were going as far as Oyster Bay, then being taken off on a pilot boat. I enjoyed the burst of surprise and envy when I answered the inevitable question with "No, I'm not getting off at Oyster Bay. We're taking the ship to Naples."

Joe Gerson, a spry old gent in a baseball cap emblazoned EMPIRE STATE—1949–1999, had been on my father's cruises and knew a lot of the same people, such as third mate Bill Hawley.

"Bill Hawley was my rabbi," Gerson said. "He was a great guy. He was my rabbi, Mr. Hawley. Without Bill Hawley I would never have made it. I remember him telling me as if it were today, 'Every stevedore carries a tin cup. Have a drink with him. You'll get more with a little booze than with the vinegar. Remember: be a Third Mate and act the part. Always be in the swim. Never be out of the swim. . . .' "

At that moment the ship's horn blasted and the pier began to move away. I checked my watch: 10 A.M. We were leaving. I clanged up the metal stairway to the bridge and scanned the huge crowd lining the shore. My friends had said they might take the bus up from Manhattan, but we hadn't found each other. I couldn't believe they'd actually make the trip, but waved energetically toward land anyway, just in case. Admiral David C. Brown, the head of the school, was leaning against the rail, watching the fort recede. "You will notice," he observed, "that the ship left promptly at 10 A.M."

I nodded, thinking: *a complete anti-climax*. The second dramatic high point of the morning shot to hell. I didn't even know where my father was at the moment. That's why it is bad to anticipate. The times you imagine are going to be significant fall flat, while excitement boils up where it isn't expected. Whatever this trip is going to offer, I thought, won't be in the departure. Still, I kept my eyes on the skyline of New York City as it waned, feeling very much out of the swim, wondering how things would be by the time Charleston—our first stop—loomed into sight. The people on the dock were tiny dots, interrupted by bunches of balloons. *That's* what the balloons were for: so those on board could spot their families and loved ones, could cling to the sight of them as long as possible as the ship sailed away.

All the first day, my father and I explored the ship, at first together and then splitting up. Living in a world of general flimsiness, of thin sheet metal and plastic bumpers, all designed to just barely work and no more, I found a real thrill in the overengineering of a ship, basically a fifty-story building designed to lie on its side and be pounded by the might of the ocean.

I wandered, delighting in just how solid everything was. In the bow, twin capstans to pull up the anchors—a pair of 12,000-pound, two-pronged black monsters. The capstans were huge spools, three feet wide and made of a brass alloy that you could tell, just by tapping with a knuckle, was something far denser and stronger than the fragile substances typically encountered on shore.

The links of the anchor chain were eight inches long, shaped like the numeral 8, the center stud to prevent tangling. Bolts as thick as forearms were secured by nuts as big as fists. I went to the bridge, a wide, shallow room at the top of the ship, glassed in on three sides that offered a view of the long foredeck. The king posts—a large square of metal beams, framing the sky—had four long booms hanging from them, cranes left over from the ship's days as a freighter. A grove of blowers supplying fresh air and venting the lower levels that led to an expanse of open deck, painted dark green, flanked by lifeboats.

A cadet stood at the helm, which was not a grand wooden spoked wheel like in the pirate movies, but small—the size of a dinner plate. The tiny wheel lent a certain air of delicacy to the act of piloting the ship, like an immense chef cracking a quail's egg. Other cadets—maybe half a dozen—stood at charts and at the two new, colorful Raytheon radar stations. I slipped behind the helmsman and watched, quietly.

Perhaps fifteen seconds later, my father appeared in the starboard doorway, a look of concern etched on his face. I smiled at him. He made an abrupt, "come here" gesture. I went there.

"You're on the bridge," he whispered, deadly earnest.

"I know," I whispered back. "That's where I can see what's going on."

"The captain won't like it," my father warned.

"Let's see," I said. I turned around and walked over to the man who was obviously Captain Joseph Ahlstrom—the tall, pleasant-faced officer with sandy hair whom everybody was listening to. I introduced myself. We shook hands. "Do you mind if I'm on the bridge?" I said.

"Make yourself at home," the captain said, in a strong Staten Island accent. Flashing my father an "easy-as-pie" shrug, I returned to my spot behind the helm. When I next looked in my father's direction, he was gone.

The bridge was a jumble of technologies, new and old. Opposite the helm was a square box showing the ship's heading in red LED numerals. Next to the box, a brass clock that the navigator wound once a week with a little brass key. At the far left—the port—was the Global Maritime Distress and Safety System that, with the touch of a button, would send a mayday message around the world. The ship had a radio operator because the state required one, but it really didn't need him. The satellites will protect us. Behind the helm were speaking tubes to the captain's quarters and the radio room. The tubes had brass mouthpieces.

It took a while for my father to actually step inside the bridge, and when he did, he ventured in tentatively, as if expecting snakes. It was a different world from when he was a sailor, and he never quite adjusted to it.

I left the bridge and returned to wandering, stepping through high doorways, over chains. At the very end of the ship—the stern—I stood on the fantail and watched the foamy white trail of the ship bubbling behind us, spreading out. A cadet always stood watch at the stern, on the platform above the supply house, facing backward, to make sure some careless faster ship didn't sneak up unnoticed on the *Empire State* and ram her. That, and as a final, desperate hope to anybody who fell overboard. I studied the churning surf passing behind the ship, focusing on a particular bit of foam and counting. It moved away fast. You'd have about five seconds to catch that lookout's attention. Then it would just be you, alone, in the vast, wide, deep ocean.

I wondered what I wanted out of this trip. People do not change. I firmly believed that. My father and I would come to no understandings. The past would remain enigmatic. Nothing would be solved. No hugs at the happy ending, eyes wet with love and reconciliation. No epiphanies. No life's lessons learned. We would end up, I was certain, exactly as we began, shaking our fists at each other as the taxicabs screeched away in opposite directions.

That's what I told myself. But it was a lie, a protective fiction concocted to soften the impact of what I feared would happen to my unspoken hopes. In my heart I wanted everything to work out—to salve the old wounds, to discover something new, to find a better, more genuine father beneath the one I knew too well, to craft myself into the son he truly wanted. I was a fool and, like most fools, believed that I was wise.

I hadn't liked my father in so long that it took effort—an act of will, leaning on the rail, gazing at the ocean, and remembering—to draw myself back to a time when I had liked him.

My earliest memories are of steamy bathrooms, the croup, and of my father wrapping me in a soft orange, yellow, and red blanket and carrying me to the hospital late at night. As I child I was often sick. Fevers, ear infections, strep throat, mumps, chicken pox. During the long days of recuperation, my father would entertain me. He found a toy monkey on a unicycle that traveled across a string and strung it over my bed. He spangled the ceiling of my room with glow-in-the-dark stars and planets and comets.

Dad would sit next to my bed at a metal TV tray and build models. Not cars or ships, but educational models. Dinosaurs—a brontosaurus, a stegosaurus, *Tyrannosaurus rex*. And anatomy models—the Visible Head, the Visible Man. He would work at them for hours, silently, a fine brush in his hand, adding the tiniest details: small red veins in the eyeballs in the Visible Head, hair on the legs of the Neanderthal man, shiny blue enamel lungs and a pink brain for the Visible Man. They were beautiful.

Those models established my earliest view of my father as a man who could do anything. He had every tool imaginable—a timing light and a belt sander and a set of German drafting instruments nestled in green velvet. He had tiny jeweler's screwdrivers and a variety of sledge-hammers, mallets, and a pickax. A jigsaw and a circular saw and a coping saw and a rip saw. He built not only models but also bookshelves, easels, cabinets, and a pair of rooms at the end of the house. I was seven when he constructed them and I was thrilled one winter morning when he handed me a claw hammer and showed me how to pull the old bent nails out of the cedar boards he was stripping from the side of the house where the new rooms would be. Later I realized that those rooms were better built than the house itself.

When I was eleven, there was the capstone: a two-story structure at the back of our yard. We called it "the Shed," but it was really a lovely, tight A-frame cabin of his own design, with a tongue-in-groove floor, a steeply sloping roof, a skylight, a large area to store equipment below and, up a ladder and through a trap door, a secret clubhouse just for my brother and me. He built it alone, except for the day a neighbor helped set the heavy beams in the roof. Construction took two weeks, and he did it while I was away at summer camp, so it would be a surprise.

This was the bedrock of my feelings for my father. He was a man of skill and surprise. He was a smart man, a scientist, who worked at NASA while my friends' fathers were mechanics and janitors. He once brought a ruby laser home from the lab, and we had fun shining the tiny red dot on the leaves of trees across the street. I fired it at the moon and imagined the light arriving. He showered me with shoulder patches from the *Apollo* moon flights, and I was the only person I ever met who had his own Van de Graaff generator to play with at home.

Our house was filled with books. Hundreds and hundreds of them, which I did not realize was exceptional until I got older and would visit the homes of friends, where I would proceed from room to room with growing amazement, wondering where their books were. The idea that they didn't have any was hard for me to grasp, at first.

My father wasn't just brainy. He was physical, comforting, and fun. He ran, he chased, he wrestled. In the winters, he built an enormous ice skating rink in our backyard. In the summers, before I learned to swim, he would hold me in the brilliant blue-white of the Berea Pool, and coo "ba-doomp, ba-doomp" as he bobbed up and down in the sparkling cold water. He would play Herb Alpert's "Tijuana Taxi" on the hi-fi, loud, and we would all dance madly. My sister and I brushed his hair; we connected the freckles on his back; we played with the flab at his waist. He announced that his big bed was a ship about to set sail, and we would come running with shrieks and throw ourselves onto it, delighted.

Then it all stopped, for reasons mysterious. The ensuing years obscured those feelings, that foundation, like silt building up on an ocean floor, until the layers became so thick that for long stretches I forgot what was below.

The models became broken through lack of care and eventually were thrown away. The stars were scraped off the ceiling. I became an adolescent and no longer wanted to help him in his projects. When pressed, I would stand in the driveway, slump shouldered, gazing dully at the ground as he lectured about some dull chore—tuning the carburetor—the details wafting over me and lost, immediately. We fought and bickered and sulked.

I collected his failings with a philatelist's care. He was timid; he wouldn't let me put a McGovern bumper sticker on the car in 1972, citing the Hatch Act, incorrectly. There were moments of rage—the occasional slap, such as when I told him that I had heard enough of his tales of his father, and he should go tell the rocking horse. The slap exploded white against my eye. Or the time he tore up a stuffed animal of mine, or shattered a Royal Dalton bowl of china flowers against the wall. He had let himself become a cog in the government. He was edgy and nervous and ungraceful. He judged people; I faulted him particularly for that.

By the time I was an adult and moved away, my view of my father had settled into a kind of bemused contempt. There was one memory—I think of it as "the Finger Incident"—that illustrates the feeling perfectly.

The edges are hazy. I had to be old enough to know what The Finger meant—say, twelve or thirteen. I was in the car, with my older sister, Debbie. My father was driving and got in a traffic altercation. I don't remember the details; somebody cut us off, probably, or perhaps my father cut somebody off. Either way, he rolled down his window and angrily held up his finger to the other driver and shouted "Up yours, buddy!" His index finger. The wrong finger.

To my sister and I it was not only the funniest thing in the world but also the absolute perfect embodiment of my dad, of everything we believed him to be: aggressively mistaken, conspicuously out of place, clueless in such a deep fashion that it was lovely.

That sense of condescension-clad affection lingered with me for a long time. But then, as the years continued to march on, accumulating in that shocking way that years do, the affectionate core somehow melted away, leaving only the hollow ball of condescension, slowly hardening into a carapace of scorn and a kind of clenched toleration.

It was this sphere of contempt that I packed with me on the trip, the dark thing I wanted to chisel away, to replace with something else, anything else. The foam boiled endlessly behind the churning propeller. Dad was somewhere on the ship. I went to look for him.

CHAPTER 2

The Weight of the Planet

The *Empire State* anchored off of Port Jefferson, four miles from the sea buoy, awaiting inspection by the Coast Guard. The crew raised the anchor ball, a black, sectioned sphere at the stern, to tell other ships that we weren't going anywhere and they couldn't count on us getting out of their way. Ships are like trackless trains—big, heavy objects that take a long time to get going and even longer to stop once they do. At sea, if another ship got within three miles of the *Empire State*, it was close, and people on the bridge kept a careful eye on it.

An unfamiliar place enters the mind in patches. For the first few days we absorbed one spot, then another. Our cabins were a flight below the bridge and a flight above the officers' mess, on the same level down a short hall from the officers' lounge, a spare collection of brown vinyl furniture—two chairs facing a sofa. Above the sofa, a big black-and-white aerial shot of Fort Schuyler. On the starboard wall—the right if you're facing the front of the ship—photographs of the various ships of the Maritime College, beginning with the *St. Mary*, the full-rigged, three-masted ship made of live oak that the college used when it started in 1873 as the New York Nautical School, and leading through the *Newport*, a composite gunboat-barkentine that had both sails and an engine. Then the six *Empire States*, including a shot of the *Empire State II* cruising into Venice—the same photo that had hung on the wall in my father's den for my entire life. The latest, the *Empire State VI*, began as a freighter in 1962, and was acquired by the Maritime College in 1989. The school spent $2 million turning it into a floating classroom for five hundred students, and its presence was a constant source of pride and aggravation to Maritime, a symbol of its vacillation between university and vocational school. Maritime could never quite figure out if it was primarily a college that had its own ship or was a ship that supported an appendage college.

To pass the time before inspection, the cadets drilled. Wearing yellow raincoats, they muscled blasting fire hoses forward and back. They filled the lifeboats, lowered them, and tooled around the ship.

In addition to two traditional, open lifeboats, the *Empire State* had four orange rescue capsules. I had never seen anything like them before. They had struck me as small submarines when I first boarded the ship, though I knew that couldn't be. The cadets called them "sneakers," and they did resemble big tennis shoes—fully enclosed, to protect occupants against the roughest ship-shattering seas. The cadets entered through a sliding door in the side.

I watched one of the capsules—No. 6—launched, its engine blatting through the exhaust pipe, the pipe's cap jabbering up and down. Because the capsule was enclosed, one person getting seasick inside infected the others, sending out an expanding ripple of nausea, until all but the most iron-stomached were heaving between their knees.

But I didn't know that, yet. I leaned on the rail, smiling at the lovely day, admiring the sunlight glinting off the ocean, affectionately watching this big goofy orange floating shoe as it motored around the ship.

Such is the vast gulf between doing something and watching

somebody else doing something. Things that look so pleasant from a distance can be horrible up close. I gazed at the orange life capsule on its springtime jaunt, wishing I was aboard for the ride, while those aboard, either puking or struggling not to, desperately wished to be anyplace else.

That morning, at breakfast, my father and I had sat at a small table in the officer's mess. Sunlight twinkled on the waters off Long Island Sound. The coffee on the ship was good, and we sipped. "It's amazing," I told my father.

"What is?" he said.

"I'm thinking of that picture of the *Empire State* in your den."

"And?" he said.

"And here we are." I spread my hands. We hadn't quite entered the picture on the wall. We weren't in Venice—not yet. But we were definitely aboard the *Empire State*. I had stepped into my childhood myth, cracked open the snow dome, entered the scary barn. Unlike the drill with the orange life capsules, it had been far more daunting to contemplate ahead of time than to actually do.

We talked until the officers' mess emptied out. My father explained that when he was a young man aboard the *Empire State* he felt like he was playacting—the officer from the white ship in the harbor, basking in the lingering afterglow of America's victory in World War II. It wasn't real to him, but a role. He was eventually going to return to the Bronx.

"But you didn't return," I said, and had a thought: maybe his going on the ship as a young man wasn't acting, but *practice*. Rehearsal. Telling himself that he was only temporarily leaving home lessened the sting. It made quitting the Bronx seem less permanent, less frightening, and helped whatever new, daunting situation he found himself in seem more acceptable. If he wasn't where he wanted to be in life, well, it wouldn't last forever.

People leave for two reasons. The lucky ones want to go somewhere else, a certain goal, a place, a dream. They're lucky because, when they arrive at that goal, that place, that dream, they'll at least have the fleeting impression of achieving something. The unlucky ones want to leave because they want to get away from where they are. It makes them unlucky because once they depart, they have no idea when they're arrived at their destination since they don't have one, so they tend to keep departing, emotionally if not physically.

The problem was that my father kept the idea of departing as a philosophy: we lived in the same house in Berea for twenty-seven years, yet always maintained a certain sense of bivouac. We were newcomers, outsiders by choice, poised to flee but never fleeing.

We were just pretending to live while heading somewhere better, somewhere more exciting, more real. This was just a temporary phase. It kept us on the periphery of things. We acted as if we were just passing through, only we weren't. That was our life and we didn't know it.

I wondered how much of that rubbed off on me—how much I felt myself in a walk-on role at the *Sun-Times*, unable to accept that this was real, that this was where I had ended up, not a role, not a waystation, but my lot.

For some reason, with the coffee and muffin at breakfast in the officers' mess, it seemed to me as if wisdom were being approached. And my father's smile—a fairly rare occurrence—was genuine, even warm. I looked into his eyes, and then at the bright blue water shining over his shoulder off Long Island, and realized for the first time that they were the same blue. I compared them again. Exactly the same blue.

The *Empire State* failed its Coast Guard inspection. Word swiftly percolated through the corridors. A safety valve in one of the boilers wasn't working.

Not a serious problem—a question of the ship's losing maneuverability as opposed to, say, the boiler exploding. But it was serious enough to keep the ship from leaving Long Island Sound, and thus risked delaying our arrival in Charleston.

This put my father into a panic. My mother was meeting us in Charleston. She had not been at all keen on my father leaving for six weeks. He had never left her alone that long. What would she do? What happened if she got sick? Who would be there? She had announced she would spend the first weekend down in Charleston with us. I hadn't objected: it would give my dad something to look forward to.

But with the ship still anchored off Long Island Sound on Monday while the engineers fiddled with the valve, our arrival in Charleston on Thursday afternoon was in jeopardy. My mother might show up and we wouldn't be there—which plagued my father.

While I was glad that my father had discovered consideration for my mother, late in life, I couldn't see how worrying about the situation would affect it. To me it was simple: either we'd make it to Charleston or we wouldn't. If we did, all would be fine. If we didn't, then mom would cancel her trip. If we were only going to be a little late, she could go and entertain herself until we got there. It was completely out of our hands, anyway, so why worry?

Dad wasn't buying it. He prowled the decks, wringing the latest word from anyone he found, inevitably fragmented and contradictory. Sharon Decker, the chatty, blue-eyed Maritime College English teacher with a tattoo around her ankle, passed along the rumor that we would dock at Port Jefferson for repairs. Others presented their own theories and scraps of data.

Information though, once retrieved, didn't bring my dad comfort. It just led him to a junkie scramble for the next data point. That was his way. A month before we left, my mother phoned one evening. "Your father is worried that there'll be trouble getting out of Italy," she said. "You'll come in on the ship, not get your passport stamped, and they won't let you out."

I reminded her that customs doesn't automatically stamp passports anymore—too time-consuming. You have to ask them for a stamp if you want one as a souvenir.

"I know," my mother had said. "A woman in our tour group last year wanted a stamp, and she had to ask for it."

"If he already knows that," I asked, measuring my words, fearing the answer, "then why is he worried?"

"Your father is a very worried man," my mother said. "He worries about everything."

This worried me. He had been a fountain of reservations in the months before the trip: maybe we shouldn't take the *Empire State*. Maybe we should take the *Queen Elizabeth II* instead—more pleasant that way. Maybe we shouldn't go to Florence—too many tourists. Maybe we should go to Siena instead. Maybe, maybe, maybe.

The day before we left Fort Schuyler, I had awoke in the Maritime College V.I.P. suite to find my father studying a sheaf of papers.

"Here is a list of last season's tropical hurricanes, their wind speeds and when they occurred," he said, handing over a few pages. I examined the printout: "Summary of the 1998 Atlantic Hurricane Season," beginning with *Alex* and ending with *Karl*. The list, lifted off the Internet, included damage and number of deaths. "The 1998 season will be remembered as being one of the deadliest in history," it read. But the first storm didn't begin until July 27, more than a month after our trip would have ended. It was now the middle of May. That seemed to render the rest of the information meaningless.

"Why did you bring this?" I asked.

"I have a personal interest," he said. We gazed at each other, and he seemed to sense this wasn't an adequate answer. "I have no concern, none whatsoever," he blustered, while I looked steadily at him. "It doesn't bother me at all," he continued. "I just like to be aware, as much as I can."

* * *

OUT TO SEA

Fleeing my father's secondhand parsing of the valve situation, I headed down to the engine room, where I could fret first hand and watch them fiddle with the thing. The engine room managed to be big and cramped at the same time, a large windowless space packed with pipes and conduits and catwalks and pumps, some wrapped in soft white insulation, looking like Claes Oldenburg sculpture, others painted industrial pale green. Big red screw valves, chains leading a story or two above into the maze of ladders and tanks, hot and noisy, but not unbearably so.

I found the captain, along with chief engineer Ron Jackson and the top engineers, gathered in front of the boiler head. Everyone was looking at an array of salad-plate-sized gauges, trimmed with an inch of brass, that reflected various pressures within the boilers. They were in the midst of testing the valve, bringing the boiler up to pressure and seeing if the safety tripped properly. The black arrow on a gauge did a slow creep upward—at 750 there was a loud hiss, and the Number 4 light blinked from green to red, signaling the boiler had shut off.

A siren sounded.

"We'll try it again," said Jackson.

They tried it again. The boiler shut down automatically every time the safety tripped, so it needed to be relit. A cadet knelt and lit a long, cattail-like torch, twirling it to make sure the fire caught all around, then shoved it into the burner.

"Like lighting a stove," the captain said.

When the pressure built to 750, there were four puffs, and the gauge fell a little.

"That's how it's been all day," a cadet said. The captain crossed his arms.

"The original safety valve didn't work at all," said a cadet.

The cadets wore blue jumpsuits with their names on the back and blue helmets, which were inevitably cracked, the cracks stitched with copper wire, a Frankenstein effect.

Attempt number sixteen ended in a series of steamy staccato pops.

"That theory didn't work," said the Coast Guard inspector.

Nothing they did to the valve worked. Later that evening, I stumbled into a meeting the captain was holding in the officers' lounge, reviewing the situation. The captain said he hoped to be in Charleston by Friday morning at the latest, but he was content for the entire cruise to take place within Long Island Sound, if need be. He must have been joking, I told myself, but it was said very matter-of-factly.

I reported the news about Friday morning back to my father and, unable to stop myself, included the captain's crack about conducting the cruise within the Sound. My father sank deeper into his funk over the valve, expounding on the immensity of time we've been aboard: three whole days. Trying to calm him, I suggested that if we were still there on Thursday, he could go ashore in the running boat—which had been going to Port Jefferson every day, picking up newspapers and such—then catch a plane to Charleston and wait there with mom until the ship arrived. Problem solved.

"Who'll pay for it?" he replied.

"Don't be dense," I snapped, immediately sorry for being rude, explaining that I meant, since I was paying for every jot on the trip—plane tickets, hotel rooms, meals; that was our deal—it followed that of course I would pay for this, too, if it became necessary. My father took exception to the idea that I was paying for everything on the trip—his cab ride to the airport in Denver, for instance. He pointed out I hadn't paid for *that*. But not to worry, he said. I would. When this was over he would send me a bill.

I couldn't have been more amazed if he said, "Hey, look at this," and then, squeezing his eyes shut and going "Nnnnnggg," had levitated six inches off the floor. My father was going to send me a bill for his cab ride to the airport in Denver. Because, you see, I hadn't paid it. Yet.

Three days at sea, and still off Long Island, including the two days in New York before the ship sailed—the fifth out of forty-two. I thought to myself, following my father's lead and counting the days for the first time. More than 10 percent. But not enough. How would I get through this? I missed my wife, my two boys, my home, even my job. Suddenly this trip seemed like a very bad idea. The only thing to do was to go to bed and hope things looked better in the morning.

Things looked better in the morning. They invariably do. It has to be hormonal. Life's prospects do not generally repair themselves overnight. But the body does, our store of hope and energy—depleted during the struggles of the day—refilled and ready the next morning.

Or maybe it's just the coffee.

There was also good news. The captain announced that the ship would be getting under way. He was vague about whether the valve was actually fixed; it turned out it wasn't. The Coast Guard basically shrugged and passed the ship, based on promises to get the valve fixed as soon as they could.

I ran into Chris Zola, the first mate, in the main stairway. He told me the burial at sea would be tomorrow: they were burying the father-in-law of Karen Markoe off Long Island. Markoe, head of the Maritime College humanities department, had done the heavy lifting to get us on the ship. You can't just show up and drag your dad aboard a state university training ship. Conversations are required. Letters. It ended up a flat-out swap—they allow my father and myself on the boat, I teach a journalism course to the cadets as we cross the ocean. No problem. I had never taught a class before, but was confident. How difficult could it be?

Markoe had asked me to be there for the burial, both as a witness and, being a Jew, to say Kaddish, the prayer for the dead, over his ashes. I said yes of course I would.

At 4:30 P.M., my father and I went forward to see the anchor raised.

Water cascaded from the chain as it was winched through the hawse-pipe and into the ship. We were under way.

At dinner we sat with the librarian, Mr. Folcarelli, a tidy older gentleman with curly black pomaded hair and prominent teeth. He seemed to take the job seriously, posting clippings from the *New York Times* about Charleston and setting out tourist guides so the cadets would know their way around.

The librarian said he was a retiree and asked my father if he was working or retired.

"I spend my days painting," my dad said, which struck me as airy and pretentious and a lie. I knew he hadn't painted a picture in the past six months. He hadn't even brought a sketchbook or paints on board.

I kept my mouth shut, but it gnawed at me. I knew a guy in college, Mark Bishko, one of those *faux artiste* types who wore the right eye-glasses that all the *faux artiste* types were wearing at the moment and cultivated an air of Oscar Wildean languor in lieu of actually doing anything creative.

Once, I casually asked Bishko what he was up to. His response, delivered in a fey, orchid-sniffing sigh, was: "I spend my days writing poetry . . . in Italian . . . about the snow."

That had retired the Poseur Prize for years, though "I spend my days painting" offered competition. Maybe it was just the way the sentence was constructed that bothered me. Any activity tacked on after "I spend my days . . ." will sound pretentious. "I spend my days . . . in a factory . . . packing boxes." Maybe that was it.

I struggled not to say anything. But the next day I was still brooding, and decided the only way to move on was to say my piece and be done.

"Why not just say 'I'm retired'?" I asked my father. What was wrong with being retired? I'd love to be retired. Had he painted a picture all year? What was he ashamed of?

Nothing, he said. His airbrush was broken and he needed a part to fix it, that's all. I thought: *your airbrush is broken? Boo-hoo. When Matisse's hands were too crippled by arthritis to hold a brush, he held it in his mouth.*

I let it go. I was trying not to be the stern accuser all the time. I looked at the pictures of Ross and Kent I had brought with me and imagined the horror I would feel, after surviving years of endless, head-crushing, gerbil-on-a-wheel parental effort, only to have them turn and condemn me, a pair of angel-faced Torquemadas. Sorry, Dad; good try, but not good enough.

The horror I *will* feel. That is inevitable. Fathers by definition let their sons down. They have to. They can't live up to expectations because the expectations grow as large as they can. If you bring home a pony on Tuesday and another on Wednesday, by Thursday your sons will greet you at the door with: "Where's the pony?" Children will expect whatever you can do and a little more. Or a lot more. I remember walking down the street with Ross when he was about two. He was at that phase where he asked the names of the passengers in every passing airplane and where they were going. This time he noticed, for some reason, the streetlights lining the block.

"Turn them on, Daddy," he said, smiling up at me, bright and expectant. I hesitated, trying to postpone the inevitable, glancing up at the row of streetlights, wondering for an insane moment if perhaps there wasn't a way. . . . Otherwise, it seemed the first step in a very long slide. "I'm sorry, honey," I finally whispered. "I can't." Ross must have forgotten it the next minute, but I chewed on the exchange for a long time. The disappointment process had begun.

I went up to the bridge after dinner to watch the ship being navigated. Evening fell. I leaned on the rail on the starboard bridge wing—an open area just outside the bridge. We passed Plum Island, an ominous federal outpost for studying animal diseases, forbidden to the public.

The darkening grayish-green sea blurred with the horizon, smudging together where they met, a pastel smeared by God's thumb.

I went down to the room and got into bed to read. At 10 P.M. there was a rap on the door. I got up to open it—in my boxer shorts and a T-shirt. I didn't bring pajamas, haven't worn them in years. There was the captain. Just a reminder, he said, we'll be burying Sam Markoe at sea tomorrow at 6 A.M. I told him I'd be there.

That night, the *Empire State* sailed into heavier seas, a "beam sea," meaning that the waves, blowing in from the southeast, hit the ship on the side, causing her to roll.

Lying on my back in my bunk, it was as if an unseen hand was reaching out from under the mattress, pulling first on my left shoulder, then on the right. There was a ghostly shifting and clanking all around the darkened room. Unsecured items kept crashing to the floor. A can of shaving cream boomed into the bathtub and rolled around until I got up, picking my way blindly to stow it. I peered at my father in the darkness. He seemed to be asleep.

The night passed that way. After midnight I heard voices in the hall. They continued for a while. I assumed the voices were others from nearby cabins, also unable to sleep, gathering to talk. I pulled my pants on, thinking to join what I imagined as a happy slumber party scene, and went blinking into the eternal daylight of the corridor. The conversation turned out to be coming from five cadets, relaxing on their mops and buckets, chatting outside our door. They saw me and got back to swabbing. I returned to the room. I suppose at some point I slept.

At 7 A.M.—an hour later than planned—we buried Sam Markoe at sea. The morning was foggy off Barnegat Bay, a section of the New Jersey coastline dotted with whimsically named spots such as Little Egg Harbor and Point Pleasant Canal. The captain wore his salt-and-pepper uniform. My father and I met him on the bridge. Along with

Sharon Decker, representing the humanities department, and Jim McCabe, the web site reporter, we trooped back to the fantail, the captain in the lead, holding a small black box. The sun was a dim whitish yellow disk in the fog directly over the flagpole at the stern.

Before leaving, I had spoken to Markoe's son, Arnie, so I knew a little bit about the man in the box. He had spent his career selling Arrow shirts, going back to the days when they came with detachable collars. But I didn't mention that. Instead I spoke, generally, of his love for the sea and his love of fishing. "He was a good man," I said. I didn't know this as a fact, but his son had gotten choked up talking about him, and that is as sure a sign as any. Besides, it was my experience that most men are good men, and even if they are not, they become good men once they're gone. No one wants to profane the dead.

I sure don't—that was a big reason I wanted to figure out my dad while he was still here. I saw how his father's death, in 1963, when my dad was thirty, had left him angry and bewildered, fencing with the air, carrying on a one-way argument with the dead. He would deny this, but it was clear to me the way he clung to and relived the various secondary hurts of his father's passing—that my mother phoned him at work with the news, rather than wait until he got home, so he could cry in private. That his brother Morty sold off, without consulting him, their father's beloved stamp collection. The vague possibility of medical incompetence. My father harped on every wrong, I eventually realized, except the central one: that his father had shrugged and left the scene abruptly, without explaining, without a good-bye, dropping dead in the street and never providing the blessing or showdown or resolution my father sought. I looked at my father, his hair tousling in the breeze. Whatever emotions I had were so submerged—black eels slithering through the dark mud a mile below the frozen surface of an Arctic sea—that I couldn't even speculate what they might be.

The captain poured the silvery ashes into the silvery sea. I began to recite the Kaddish—*"Va yiska dal, va yiska dash, shme rabba. . . ."* I had realized with anxiety, the night before, that for all the times I've said the prayer in synagogue, I didn't really have it memorized, and hadn't brought a Hebrew prayer book with me. I'd have to wing it. After practicing several times beforehand, I thought I was able to reconstruct a good deal of the solemn prayer, particularly at the beginning. But that morning on the fantail some of it came out condensed and garbled, and some was merely gibberish. As I stumbled over the words I thought of tradition faded by time and assimilation, mangled and creolized by people such as myself, who didn't hold it in high enough regard to get it right. Five thousand years of Jews suffering and dying to hand a tradition down to me, so I could open my fingers and let it blow away on the wind. Nobody noticed, certainly not my father. I told myself God wouldn't mind—nothing much seems to bother Him nowadays. I finished just as the last of the ashes hit the water, with the standard English, "May the God of peace bring peace to those who mourn and comfort the bereaved among us."

The captain saluted the waters and ordered two blasts on the ship's horn. A few of us shook hands and the ceremony was over. At that moment, as if on cue, the sun broke through the clouds and flashed brilliantly against the white waters swirling behind the ship.

My father used my IBM Thinkpad to write an e-mail to my mother— just a basic, love-ya-see-ya-Friday message—and I transferred it to a disk so he could take it to the radio operator. But the radio operator, a bespectacled, pot-bellied career seaman from San Diego named Roger Groeper, couldn't send it. He said he had trouble with the satellite e-mail system. It was brand new, filled with glitches, and sent information at a molasses-off-a-stick-in-winter crawl of 35 baud, more than a thousand times slower, literally, than my computer at home. So problems could be expected. But my father sniffed conspiracy. Roger didn't *want* to do it. He was afraid that if he sent this one, my father speculated, he'd have to send one "every week."

While he wrestled with the matter I excused myself to go to class. Teaching journalism had turned into a bigger hassle than I initially imagined. The first class had begun on our first night on the ship: nineteen young faces staring up, blank and expectant, following me tropistically, like flowers tracking the sun, as I paced sweating back and forth at the front of the windowless, belowdecks classroom. A few of the faces were bright, a few were dull; there were a couple Marines and a couple of unnervingly pretty girls. All had other classes, plus ship's duties, watches, and projects—so much work that they could barely do the minimal writing I assigned. I hadn't talked to teenagers in fifteen years and wasn't sure how to do it anymore. I tried to be prepared, but I would blow through two hours of material in twenty minutes. The result wasn't pretty.

Still, it was a place to escape to, and with my father analyzing the details of the e-mail conspiracy, I fled to my class, arriving to find a developing crisis. I had been so understanding of the demands my students faced that only one student out of nineteen bothered to show up, along with the ship's doctor, John Richardson, a New Hampshire urologist, tanned and hearty with wavy white hair. He had heard the class was interesting. I was flattered that he stopped by but embarrassed by the turnout. I taught for thirty-five minutes and then called it quits.

After class I went to watch the sun set from the bridge. Captain Ahlstrom joined me and we got to talking. He grew up on Staten Island—he used to watch the oceangoing ships pass under the Verrazano-Narrows Bridge from the window of his high school. He went to Maritime and put out to sea, serving on freighters and bulk carriers, toting up adventures in ports around the world. He was filled with colorful tales of salty dogs who brawled with fire axes.

The captain made a point to golf in every port. He asked me if I golfed. I said no. The only time I had ever been on a golf course was following Arnold Palmer around eighteen holes in Montego Bay,

Jamaica, for a magazine profile. "He wasn't having fun and he's really good at it," I said. "I figured I probably wouldn't have much fun at it, either." He asked if my father golfed. Golf was so far removed from my father's character that I had never paired the two concepts—my father and golf—in a single thought before. I had to smile. It was as if the captain had asked if my father took heroin or danced the tango.

Ahlstrom was very aware that his style was a change of pace for people weaned on Captain Olivet and others like him. He said he'd yell at cadets more if he thought they needed it for their careers at sea, but they don't. He wanted them to have a good experience on the *Empire State*, not to remember it as a time when they were always being chewed out. I returned to the room, buoyed by the conversation. The captain seemed like a decent egg.

"Hey Dad," I said, preparing to recapitulate our talk.

My father cut me off with a look. "Sharon Decker is sending the ship's web page via e-mail," he said. He was being lied to. Dark forces were afoot.

I had no sympathy. If anyone should worry about the e-mail, it was me. I had nine columns to get back to the *Sun-Times* to make up for my not stockpiling enough to cover my absence. I figured I would mail a few from Charleston as a backup and then test the e-mail on ship on the way down to Barbados. Protective redundancy; if the e-mail didn't work, the snail mail would. And if e-mail worked, I would have the entire ocean voyage to file. If it didn't, I would have to file most of them from Barbados and the rest the moment I hit Italy. However it worked out, it would be fine.

My father couldn't think that way. He lurched from one fixation to the next. First it was leaving Port Jefferson, and now that we were steaming toward Charleston, he was obsessed with the e-mail. When that resolved itself he will turn his focus—I realized, grimly contemplating the situation again as I lay in bed, listening to the engines thrumming through the darkness—on some new problem.

* * *

We awoke Friday morning to find ourselves anchored off the port of Charleston, waiting so the ship would steam in precisely at the 10 A.M. arrival time. That was important—a 565-foot ship can't just show up whenever it wants and parallel park. You need tugs, a pilot, people ashore to catch lines.

The pilot boat approached. Every port big enough to merit the name has a pilot, or several, whose job it is to guide ships in. The pilot arrives on a small speedboat, boldly marked PILOT in huge letters. The pilot boat pulls alongside the ship, which slows but does not stop. The pilot leaps aboard, generally—every few years one miscalculates his step and lands in the drink. Pilots are treated with respect bordering on deference. They are liaisons to the port and, not incidentally, the people who must by law guide the ship back out again. The savvy captain will press a couple of cartons of cigarettes on the pilot, or invite him to dinner, or—after the ship is docked—drinks, or whatever else the tradition at that particular port demands. Any whiff of corruption is blown away in the typhoon of practicality: do you want your ship's schedule thrown off twelve hours or a day or three over a carton of cigarettes?

I stood on the left wing of the bridge. Two beige-and-white tugboats, the *Christopher B. Turecamo* and the *Carly A. Turecamo*, came alongside to guide the *Empire State*. They were, I noticed, exactly the same yellowish brown as both the classrooms and the ship's kingposts, an ugly color I dubbed "nautical beige."

The port of Charleston was old, bustling, with historic homes and a large commercial shipping facility spread out in a wide vista. There was a marina, a span of bridge, a boatyard with large blue-and-white cranes. The sky was clear, cloudless, bright, bright blue. Ahead was a warehouse area and grand old porch-fronted homes. Entering the harbor, I used the doctor's binoculars to examine Fort Sumter, a rather low and unpromising pile of bricks passing to port. To our starboard was the aircraft carrier *Yorktown*. That looked more interesting. "Maybe we should go aboard," I told my father.

"I've seen her," he said. "Or an aircraft carrier like her."

As we neared the wharf, Dad suggested we should perhaps get off the bridge "and give the captain room." I looked around—in addition to ourselves, on the port wing were Doc Richardson, smoking a pipe, and an elderly professor, Hap Parnham, who is easily six foot two. There were another dozen people inside the bridge house, and the captain, maybe twenty feet away from us, wasn't even directing the ship—that's what the pilot was for. It amazed me that my dad would feel conspicuous and want to go below just when something interesting was happening.

I draped my right arm around my father's shoulders. "You're just as good as anyone else, Dad," I said. He smiled.

"Almost," I added, unable to resist.

I could pick out my mother on the pier from a great distance, when the people there still looked about the size of grains of rice, from her electric-blue blouse and the way she stood, hands grasping forearms as if she were trying to hold in her excitement.

My mother—what can you say? Of course I love her. She was the metronome that kept our family running, always suggesting projects and planning activities, the giddy counterpoint to my father's clenched personality. For all my dad's romantic dreams of action, it was she who really did things—who planned the vacations, bought tickets to the plays, to the concerts, who dragged my father, grumpy and complaining, into the world. When they moved to Colorado, it was she who joined the Eskimo Club and learned to ski, or tried to. True, she fell on her first run down the hill, broke her leg in three places, and never skied again. But she tried.

It was she who took me to the library, gave me activities when I was bored, told me that my father didn't mean it, that he was saying he was sorry in his own way. She who put up with him and kept the family together. Later, when I was a teenager, it was she who would take us to the Brown Derby by the airport, after dropping my father off for one of his frequent jaunts abroad. "Mr. International Coast-to-Coast Bigshot," I called him, derisively. We would sit, waiting for our steaks, liberated, gleeful, practically toasting his plane with our apricot sours as it roared away overhead. Free, for two weeks.

She was forged in the stiletto-heel femininity of the late 1940s and early 1950s, a time of girdles and Cuss Banks and fire-engine-red lipstick. Her mother, my Grandma Sarah, was something of a dame, a clerk at the May Company department store and star of her world of poker-playing, choir-singing Jewish ladies.

My mother loved music; she was a singer in the U.S.O., who went to Europe to entertain the troops when she was seventeen. This was in 1953. I couldn't help but note that while my father chugged across the ocean in an old, decommissioned Navy transport ship, struggling to master a technology that even then was about to disappear, my mother flew across the Atlantic in a new U.S. Army Super Constellation to sing "A Stormy Day." She was a content provider while my father was a glorified human circuitbreaker.

Once, when my parents came to visit me in Chicago, I took them to Andy's, a jazz club near the newspaper office. As genuine a place as you can imagine—old and airy, with a big wooden horseshoe bar and banners from every jazz festival going back twenty years hanging from the brick walls. Some combo grooving on the small stage. We sat at the bar and listened. Then my mother excused herself—I assumed to visit the restroom. The next thing we knew, she was up on stage with the band, singing "Goody, Goody."

That's my mother. And the great part of that evening is my father for once rolled with it. He didn't flinch. I watched him watching her sing, absorbed, smiling, love in his eyes, as if connecting back to deeper, subterranean rivers of emotion.

My father's characteristic response would have been to cringe. When I took my family to visit them in Colorado, the March before my father and I left on the ship, my mother and father were on the couch in their living room, and a neighbor came within sight of the back door. My mother leapt up, threw open the door, and called to the neighbor to come meet her son and his family. My father actually turned his body away from the door, rolled his eyes at me, and ducked his head, reeling as if embarrassment had struck him a physical blow.

Everything knotted and strained in myself is my father's legacy, and everything light and fun and impulsive is my mother's. It's a bad mix in some ways because the mother in me is always leading me into reckless acts that the father in me then agonizes over and regrets.

She liked being the center of attention—I suppose we all do—and it irked her that my father and I were going on this trip without her. Perhaps, she told me, the people on the ship would be so impressed with her when she visited in Charleston that they'd insist she remain aboard all the way to Italy. A typical piece of motherly fancy, but also a hint at how disappointing the world must be, frequently, to someone who can entertain thoughts like that.

I worried she would beg my father to return: that was my secret fear. They were staying at her hotel. I feared she would work on him and, come Sunday, he'd vanish back to Colorado. Again, I had it exactly backward.

A thermonuclear sun was rising over Charleston harbor. The *South*, I thought, walking into town to meet my parents. I passed a tall man in a straw hat with a colorful band, and was surprised when he greeted me. "Hello, Captain," I said, recovering at the last moment. Captain Ahlstrom had one of those pleasant, round faces that doesn't have any particular distinguishing characteristic, and several times, when I saw him in different settings or different outfits, it took me a moment to realize who he was.

My parents and I were rendezvousing at Kahal Kadosh Beth Elohim, a historic Romanesque synagogue on Hessal Street. Though it was Saturday morning, I hadn't considered that the synagogue might be in use, assuming it would be a museum. I wore a green pocket T-shirt and shorts.

Well-dressed Charlestonians milled about the pillars in front of the synagogue. Everyone was in suits and summer dresses. A boy was about to be bar mitzvahed. Trying to squeeze myself into a smaller, less noticeable shape, I slid up to an usher, who told me to come back tomorrow and I could see the inside. I stood outside the iron fence, gazing down the street.

The folks arrived and marched into the service. I felt inhibited and hung back. I'll wait outside, I said, but my father returned and pressed me to come in with them. Inside was a classical, square sanctuary, with cream-colored walls and ornate, wedding-cake-frosting trim. Tall stained-glass windows, colorful geometric patterns of green, pink, blue, and brown. The ark—dark polished wood, circular—slid open to reveal green velvet curtains.

I had time to study the congregation, which didn't fill a quarter of the fine wooden pews, the women in hats, several beautiful teenage girls, and a little boy in a costly, one-piece plaid playsuit with tall socks, an ensemble that I had seen in movies and fashion photographs but never on an actual child in the living world.

The bar mitzvah boy was appropriately freckled, bemused and gangly. His grandfather presented a prayer shawl and told him of being informed of his father's birth while fighting in the woods in Germany. When I had my bar mitzvah, my father's father, Sam, had been dead for a decade and Irving, my mother's father, a stolid Pole, wasn't the sort to make speeches.

Mom sang along, humming with the cantor, loudly—the only person to do so. After about fifteen minutes, she leaned over and said we could leave anytime I wanted. I let a minute or two pass, gave the nod, and we got up and left. Walking out—not quite far enough out for my tastes—my mother announced that she couldn't stand a synagogue where the congregation didn't sing.

I understood exactly what she meant. What's the point, if you're not going to sing?

None of the tensions I expected developed from the weekend with my mother. We visited tourist sites, ate in restaurants, even saw a movie. In the evenings my parents retired to the hotel and I hit the town. The Sunday we left Charleston, I met my parents for a breakfast of crabcakes, poached eggs, and fresh Bloody Marys. People were dressed for church. I always thought those Ralph Lauren ads were a lie, but in whatever direction I looked, my gaze settled on men in white linen jackets and ladies wearing muslin dresses and sunhats. I'd swear I also saw children in sailor suits and knickers, rolling hoops with sticks. But that has to be a trick of memory.

On the street, we said good-bye to my mother. She was staying for the rest of the day, heading off to tour a historic home. I hugged her, then stepped away and stood at a discreet distance, gazing off while she and my father said their farewells.

Then it was he and I, alone together again, walking toward the ship, down Broad Street, a lovely old avenue. We were quiet, tentative, perhaps aware that the grease in our grinding gears had just drained away. The fact that the trip was about to begin in earnest had started to settle in over the weekend in Charleston. Life back home hadn't frozen in my absence; it was changing—my close friend at the paper, the Sunday editor Mark Jacob, had quit and gone across the street to the *Tribune*. "I have bad news for you" my wife had begun, and I did that tensing thing you do when you know that life's roulette wheel has spun and you're about to find out where the silver ball has landed. Mark's leaving wasn't a death, but was unexpected and it stung. Things would not be the same when I got back.

And at home? My wife, Edie—I was, if not exactly worrying about her, then thinking about her in earnest. When we parted at the airport the week before, she had given me a long, desperate, eyebrow-raising kiss—a kiss, I thought at the time, worth leaving home for. But now that I was gone I wasn't so sure. How would she hold up, with a one-year-old and a three-year-old? I phoned her from shore the hour before the ship sailed. Everything's fine, she said. Everyone's fine. They miss me, but they're fine. Then Ross came on the phone and asked why I couldn't just come home right now?

I mulled over my options. "Daddy has to go through some sort of contrived ordeal by fire with grandpa in the hope that you don't turn into half the head case your daddy is," didn't sound like something to say to a little boy. I clucked vague, positive, reassuring noises.

CHAPTER 3

The Collapse of Foam

The wind whipped off the Atlantic Ocean so strong that the signal flags spelling the *Empire State VI*'s call letters—KKFW—gave off a ripping rumble that was half blowtorch, half jet engine. The wind tore spray off the crests of the ship's wake, hurling it fizzing into a rainbow mist. The wake was a complex mix of royal blue and white bubbles, with a heart of pure aquamarine just below the surface.

That evening's class was journalism ethics. I outlined the various responsibilities of a reporter—toward the newspaper, toward the truth, toward the subject—and the various things that can influence a reporter: gifts, friendship, personal bias.

I asked the class to think about real-life cases that come up all the time. You're profiling the chef from the Ritz. She invites you and your wife to enjoy a dinner there. On the one hand, the cuisine is part of the story. On the other, you're accepting a $400 meal. Yin: the paper should pick up the tab to keep things honest. Yang: it won't.

My father sat in on the class. When I had mentioned that the doctor was attending classes, I noticed an expression cross my father's face, and I told him that he could come, too, if he wanted. I wasn't comfortable having him there—it wasn't as if he would have thought of it without the doctor's lead—but it would be wrong not to let him. During class, I didn't look in his direction.

Ethics is a tangled subject. I believe that objectivity is a myth; everybody is biased. The question is not whether a reporter has an opinion, but whether that opinion is reflected in the article. Is it fair? Is it slanted? We talked about how bias can creep into a story.

I didn't want to sugarcoat the profession, to make it a branch of public relations. Most people cannot write well, not because they can't form proper sentences but because they balk at expressing the sharp thoughts that make for good writing. They're too nice, or too timid.

This is not particular to writing. It takes a little hardness to accomplish anything. To do something worthwhile invariably abuses some aspect of a relationship, if only because you pay attention to an area you'd otherwise ignore, or you ignore someone you'd otherwise pay attention to.

Ambition is a form of treason, a kind of betrayal. You can't practice the piano and go out and play kickball with the guys at the same time. You can't both write and push somebody on a tire swing. You have to choose, sometimes. Often.

After class, my father and I returned to our cabin, climbing the several levels of stairs from the classrooms, deep in the ship. I cleared the decks for my father's praise, but it didn't come. "You talk too fast," he said. "And you use too many 'You knows.' " The real-life cases I had used as illustrations just made me seem, in his eyes, corrupt.

Too wound up from class to consider sleep, I took a book out to the officers' lounge. But it was too bright. I couldn't get comfortable on the vinyl furniture. The words danced before me. Setting down the book, I went outside and walked toward the bow, into a roaring, warm

wind. The stars were largely obscured, by a two-thirds moon. The sky
was black-orange. A cluster of air vents moaned as I went by, leaning
into the wind, which pushed me back, hard.

It was vertiginous to walk the deck, even in the center, as the
ship slowly shifted—you couldn't really call it rolling—this way and
that, with inky death rushing by just over each rail. The walk felt
eerie, dreamlike. The ship reminded me of the suspension bridges in
Cleveland—sooty industrial spans that raised and lowered and snaked
above the steel mills in the Flats, bridges that gave me nightmares as a
child. There was one dream I never forgot: I was walking on a bridge,
no rail, a step away from tumbling into the black abyss of smokestacks
below. In the dream, the section of the bridge I was on lowered, like
the deck elevator on an aircraft carrier, and I lay flat on the small
square of descending deck, in tingling terror of the edge. I never
walked to the bow of the ship at night again.

The next morning I woke up early—maybe 4 A.M. I tried to go
to sleep, counting backward, thinking calming thoughts. Nothing
worked. So shortly after 5 A.M. I got dressed and went outside to
watch the sun rise.

It was cloudy, with stormy gray billows off the port bow. The ship
was heading due southeast, into warmer water. A triangle of lightness
appeared to the east—a thin, drawn-out triangle. Over the next half
hour it turned to a brownish yellow, a normally ugly, bruiselike color
that somehow looked beautiful under the circumstances. A string of
clouds went by like circus elephants, one leading the other. There was
a patter of rain, which I ignored. The rain shrugged its shoulders and
stopped.

The triangle grew, turning from brownish to bluish yellow. It sat
just above the horizon and, as a trick of vision, seemed like a crack
opened up in the sky, offering a glimpse into an alien landscape—

sunrise on Saturn, with craters casting blue shadows and white powder blowing off the ridges of blue-gray mountains. The sky brightened, but the sun never appeared.

At 3 P.M. the water on the ship was shut off: something was wrong with the air-conditioning. But this time I didn't go below to watch them work on it. That didn't seem to be the best path. Instead, I ran into Chief Jackson, taking air on the deck. "It was the height of arrogance," he said, "to design a ship whose windows don't open."

Later in the day my father and I were reading in our room. I glanced at my watch, stood up, shoved a notebook in my pocket, and stepped to the door. Dad asked me where I was going, and I told him I was on my way to meet with a cadet from Chicago, the son and grandson of Chicago cops.

"You know," he said, "You might want to consider writing a column about him."

I paused at the door, gazing steadily at my father, eyebrows raised, mouth open, somewhat smiling, in mock surprise, waggling both fingers in his direction. He got it.

That night's class was on copyediting. I prepared a quiz and used it as a guide to go over the rudiments. Read sentences carefully. Shorten them. Sentences should make sense. Don't use a word too many times, unless it works; then you can use the same word again and again.

The class went considerably better than the previous few. I recognized a correlation between how well a class went and how much I had prepared for it. Winging it just didn't work; preparing a quiz did. It also helped that my father wasn't there—once had been enough for the both of us.

Afterward, I went up to the bridge to watch the sun set. A sorrowful descent into the sea. My father approached, with an appearance so grave I asked him what was wrong. He said the air-conditioning was off—something he had been commenting on all day. It was hot in the dining room. I had eaten there and hadn't been bothered, at least not by the heat. He was starting to strike me as one of those fossils in an old-age home, bitching that bingo night is mismanaged.

Dad was wondering if he should go to the ship's office and fill out a form, reporting the problem. I gently pointed out that, seeing as the air-conditioning had become a crisis brought on by the warm waters as we approached the Caribbean, thus reducing the efficiency of the engines and shutting down the ship's aging cooling system; given that it was already the talk of the vessel; and considering that the entire engineering department was laboring away like plow horses in 120-degree heat belowdecks, desperately trying to fix it, perhaps taking this moment to step up and officially register his dissatisfaction might not be the most appreciated move. Dad agreed. "That's the last thing in the world I'd want to do," he said. I was beginning to really worry about him. He didn't seem to be doing anything aboard ship. I was busy, preparing for and teaching classes, writing columns, running stairs, reading. But he seemed to always be looking at the same twenty-page monograph about evolutionary psychology that he had been reading for the past week.

In the months before I went on the ship, during my endless parsing of the situation before the fact, a friend at the paper, Bob Kurson, provided a vital bit of logic that steeled my will: "If you don't go, five years from now you won't remember what you did instead. It'll be lost. But if you go, it'll always be a memory you'll carry with you." It was only now, brooding at sea over how I had been led astray, led into a small cabin with my complaining father, that I realized how Kurson's logic held true for any imaginable folly. "If you just sit there, napping, you'll forget all about it. But if you leap up and lop your finger off with an axe, why, the moment will always be a crisp memory."

Late that night, I joined a bull session with Sharon Decker, my source of hot gossip on the ship. A cadet weeping over a broken love affair had taken a bite out of the chin of another cadet who had chosen the wrong moment to taunt him. The bite required thirteen stitches to close. The biter would be sent home when the ship hit Bridgetown. Lucky guy.

The jolt rolled me out of my bunk. I slammed hard against the floor, breaking my fall with my nose. The air was electric and loud. Still, I lay there for a moment until a tremendous resonating bang sent me springing to my knees. One hand tentatively investigated my gushing nose, the other groped blindly for the bedframe. I couldn't see anything.

"Shit!" I shouted, my whole head singing. I tried to stand up, but the floor seemed to twist and I fell against the bed. I looked out the window—pitch black outside, water pelting as if from a hose. I stood up, looked at my wet hand covered in blood that looked black in the darkness, then instinctively lurched toward the door. The next roll pushed me up against it and I waited, my cheek pressing the metal, until it rolled back. I flung the door open; it bammed against the bulkhead and nearly bounced closed, but I batted it away and fell into the hall.

A buzzer above my ear screamed. *"NAAAAAAAAAAHHHHHH!"*

Someone I didn't recognize—a body in khakis—blew by, and I clutched at him with the hand that wasn't on my nose.

"What? What?" I shouted, but the person pulled away from me and ran toward the main staircase. I followed, hauling myself up the stairs using all my strength, leaving a red streak on whatever I touched.

I expected the bridge to be crowded, but there was only Captain Ahlstrom, first mate Chris Zola, navigator John Ryan, and two others I didn't recognize. Nobody noticed me.

"I'm going to turn into it," Ahlstrom shouted.

"You can't," said Zola. "The ship won't make it."

A shuddering blow nearly knocked everyone over. The sea was hammering the ship, side on. I plopped on my butt, my back against the bulwark. I stayed there a moment, then hauled myself up on the handrail. I tried to look out the bridge windows, but could hardly see through the rain, even though the wipers were zipping back and forth at full speed.

"I have to," Ahlstrom replied. "We'll break apart like this."

I wanted to ask a question, thought better of it, and, timing carefully, slipped out the back in a low running crouch, in case I hit the floor again, planning to go into the radio room and ask Roger what the hell was happening.

Roger was at his post, pale as death, eyeglasses skewed, speaking into the microphone.

"Pan-pan, pan-pan, pan-pan," he said. "All stations. This is Training Ship *Empire State*. KKFW. Training Ship *Empire State*. KKFW. *Pan-pan, pan-pan, pan-pan.* We are experiencing extremely heavy weather and taking on water. We require assistance. All vessels. All stations. We have structural damage, injured. We are approximately 19.55 North, 66.3 West, 145 nautical miles northwest of Bridgetown. All stations. All ships. *Pan-pan, pan-pan, pan-pan."*

I braced myself in the doorway, staring at him. "Holy shit!" I finally said.

He looked at me and seemed about to say something, but the radio crackled.

"Empire State, Empire State, this is Coast Guard Station Fort de France. We receive but due to extreme conditions cannot provide assistance at this time. Please heave to and . . ." At that point a lurch sent me tumbling back into the hall. Not daring to stand up, I crawled back onto the bridge. The captain and others were pressed against the window. I looked out and, after a moment to let my eyes adjust and my brain process the image, I saw the front deck of the *Empire State* buried in water, the base of a wave just having rolled over it. The king post and the cranes were gone. There were *people* on the deck. I

looked around, terrified, noticing for the first time that the captain and the mate and the rest—everybody but me—were wearing their life jackets—big orange squares framing their faces.

"That's it!" Ahlstrom cried. "Everybody off. Abandon ship! Sound it! Let's go! Let's go!" He looked at me, his face a mask of strain. "What are you doing here? Where's your father?" he said. I had no idea—I had fled the cabin without even thinking of him.

"What's going on?" I asked.

"Where's your father?" he said. "You're supposed to be at your lifeboat station. Get there now!"

I turned and rushed from the bridge, down the central stairs, unwilling to go outside. The cabin deck was frighteningly empty. Back in our room, I found my dad in the dark, clinging to the mattress on the floor.

"Dad, Dad," I shouted. "The ship's sinking. We've got to get to the lifeboats."

"I can't," he shrieked, a jelly of ineffectual terror. "I'm *afraid*!"

Reaching under the bed, I hauled out his life jacket and draped it around his shoulders, then reached for my own and put it on. "Everybody's already there," I said. "We haven't much time."

Somewhere far below, a quavering groan, like metal being torn in two. I grabbed at his hands, but they were frozen claws, locked tight against mattress. I could see him, in the white-gray light from the window, staring straight ahead, dazed, not looking at me. I made my left hand into a fist and drew it back.

"Sorry, Dad," I said, and punched him as hard as I could in the jaw. It made a sound—to my surprise—exactly like those loud, meaty *thocking* noises that punches make in the movies. He went cinematically limp, like a rag doll sprawled over the mattress. With some difficulty I scooped him over my shoulder, in a fireman's carry, and balanced him with one arm while the other guided me out into the corridor, now dark, down the stairs to the main deck.

The door opened to howling wind and rain. I staggered across the deck as best I could, but only made it about ten yards before my feet went out from under me and I sprawled on the slick green metal, my father atop me. I lay there a moment. Then the black sky yielded to a patch of purple, then red, then orange. I sat up and tracked the streaks down to the bridge, where I saw, through the downpour, the figure of the captain, one arm straight over his head, the other bracing it at the forearm. He was holding a flare pistol, firing off the *Empire State*'s parachute flares—but the gale was so fierce they disappeared almost immediately.

"Steinberg!" someone shouted above the storm. I struggled to my feet, hauling my father up after me, and hurried toward the rail, where masses of cadets were huddled, swaying like palms as they clutched at a lifeline. A nearby rescue capsule rocked savagely on its davits, rolling away from the ship then slamming back hard against it. The hatch was open and someone was gesturing to me. I dragged my father over and passed him to the disembodied hands reaching out from inside the capsule.

"Steinberg!" Before stepping in, I turned to survey the ship, settling in the water now, each wave rolling over it more and more, the signal pennants reduced to rags, chains and containers and debris washing and skittering around the deck, where the EPIRB emergency signal buoys, faint glowing orange balls freed from their brackets, bobbed around crazily.

"STEINBERG!"

"Here," I said, feebly, the deadly-gale daydream receding from my mind, suddenly replaced with memories of the bright, calm deck of the *Empire State* where we had gathered for lifeboat drill; our weekly hour of standing, clad in lifejackets, shifting our weight from one foot to the other, watching the lifeboats prepared for lowering, and waiting for our names to be called.

My father had stood next to me on those drills. As always, we tried to chat, but conversation was dulled by the need to keep an ear open for our names. We stood, in our baseball caps, the required folding knives and flashlights in our pockets, grasping our life vests for support on the open deck—it was like standing on a moving subway train without holding on to anything. The drills seemed to take forever and, inspired by the mock seriousness of the exercise, my mind kept wandering over the dramatic possibilities of shipwreck and disaster. The "Saving Dad as the Ship Sinks" fantasy was a good way to pass the time, and only improved in depth and complexity each time I ran through it.

The morning we were to arrive in Barbados I transferred four new columns to a file on a disk and gave them to Roger to satellite e-mail back to the *Sun-Times*. Okay, I thought, here goes nothing. If it doesn't work, they must have FedEx, even in paradise.

After lunch, feeling very tired, I lay on the bed, dozing. When I woke up, I discovered my father sitting slumped forward in a chair, wearing a blackout mask and earplugs, apparently asleep. He looked like a figure from a 1950s fetish magazine. All that was missing was Bettie Page with a leather paddle. My first thought was to get out of there, but I was reluctant to open the door, even for a moment, lest anybody see him. After a few minutes he stirred, removed the mask, and announced that this was how he slept, every day after lunch, for nineteen to twenty-two minutes. Then he complained about the room being hot. He noted that the ringing in his ears he suffered from at home hadn't been bothering him on the ship because he wasn't taking his massive doses of vitamin B_6.

I mulled over this information, contemplating a reply. A sarcastic "Thanks for sharing, Dad" was a likely candidate, straining in its seat and waving its hand. Instead I took the opportunity to silently slip out into the hall. It was the "nineteen to twenty-two minutes" that really stuck under my skin. Such a telling detail, like his wearing a wristwatch in the bathtub so he could take his pulse, a fact redolent of his life of meticulous worry, of graphs and averages, of minute observation of his own precious self.

I wanted to go to dinner. Dad wasn't ready, and told me to go without him. I swung by the officers' lounge, where Doc Richardson was outside at the rail, gazing at the ocean. I joined him and we got to talking about our wives and our kids. We had both gone to Japan, he to visit his son, me to visit my brother, who moved there after college.

Of all the characters on the ship, I took to Dr. Richardson most. He was a craggy, New England sort, with a farm in New Hampshire. His mother's family were sea captains from Searsport, Maine. He had an ancestor on the *Mayflower*. I decided that was where his radiating calm came from: roots. My father not only didn't know what country his grandfather came from, but he didn't remember his name and didn't seem curious to find out. Dr. Richardson's father had also been a doctor. But when I asked him how that had influenced his becoming a doctor, he seemed oddly surprised by the suggestion of a link.

"I never thought about it," he said. "It was always something I just fell into."

Dr. Richardson retired two years ago. He had worked at a clinic near Dartmouth for twenty-seven years, but then the bureaucratic tide overwhelming medicine became too oppressive to bear. With no interest in writing his memoirs, and a family tradition of seafaring, Richardson decided to go to sea. He began with the 1997 cruise under the previous captain, Scott James.

"He was sort of an unhappy guy," remembered the doctor. "The ship was much grimmer under him. He had just had two little twins—his wife was trying to have kids for a long time. The kids had just been born and he had to put out to sea. So he was not really happy; always nice to me, but not as pleasant, as loose. You wouldn't wear shorts and a T-shirt. You wouldn't walk up on the bridge unless you were invited."

We kept talking as we went to dinner, but the doctor stopped by his cabin to change his glasses, so I got to the mess ahead of him. My father was sitting with two elderly engineering professors, Gus Emig and John Perry. There was only one empty seat at their table so, wanting to carry on my conversation with the doctor, I took an empty table near them—which must have seemed strange to my father, who looked over but didn't say anything.

The Doc returned and joined me. We continued talking. His son had a characteristically bizarre Japanese job: he was a spy for Kikkoman Soy Sauce, scouting out gym equipment from rival companies so Kikkoman's athletic facilities could keep up, important in the fierce competition for new hires. We compared notes about Japan.

I couldn't help but reflect again that, in the nearly three years my brother lived in Japan, I went to see him, and my mother went to see him, alone, since my father refused to go. It was a long trip and what's in Japan anyway?

After dinner I decided to go to the fantail and smoke my cigar. I had brought a big Macanudo Churchill that a friend at the newspaper had given me, and I figured, since there would be Cubans in Barbados, I should smoke it and make room for the next stogie.

I went to my room and retrieved the cigar. Heading toward the fantail, I cut through the mess, thinking I would swing by my father's table to tell him where I was going. But he was absorbed in conversation, and it seemed like a dumb bit of information to barge in and deliver. ("I'm going to go smoke this cigar now, Dad," I'd say. "Very good," he'd say, "I'll alert the media.") So I kept going, until I reached the hind end of the ship.

Evening was settling into peaceful, soft night. I leaned on the railing. The fantail was thick with cadets, smoking and mingling—it was like a college keg party without the keg. I lit the cigar without difficulty, and fell to talking with cadets as they drifted over to check out this adult teacher person suddenly in their midst. Mostly they complained—they're paying $1,700 to chip paint for two months, for two months in a sauna. A girl came up and hung on the guy I was talking to, which was a relief. Up to that point I had seen no evidence of frolic among the cadets and was beginning to worry that either I was even more out of the swim regarding shipboard life than I already suspected or young people had gone through some fundamental change, perhaps from all those years of sitting close to computer screens and color television sets. I was glad to find evidence they hadn't. It turns out the cadets are merely discreet, by necessity.

It took nearly an hour to smoke that big cigar, and I lingered over it, enjoying the night air and the unfamiliar role of grown-up in a crowd of kids. The lights of Bridgetown drew nearer on the portside. "Pretty well lit for a Third World country," a female cadet quipped. This is fun, I thought; I'll have to come back to the fantail more often. The cigar reached its end and, with a sigh, I took a final lingering draw and flicked the glowing butt into the ocean. A lightheaded cigar buzz enveloped me pleasantly as I headed back to the cabin.

On the deck below ours I ran into the librarian. "Your father's been looking for you," he said somberly. Foreshadowing. I climbed a flight of stairs and, through the glass in the exterior door, saw my father standing outside our cabin, his face drawn with upset. I opened the door to the corridor and stepped in.

"Where the *fuck* were you?" he snapped. "You got an e-mail from your paper! A column was garbled in transmission!" He was really angry. I followed him into the room, slightly stunned, the gentle numbness from the cigar rending the cabin momentarily overlit and unfamiliar. "I was only gone an hour," I said.

He kept ranting about the e-mail, which Roger had slipped in an envelope under our door. My confusion slowly lifted. Anger is infectious; his began to bleed into me. I mustered a defense.

"They're not your bosses, they're mine," I said, hotly. "You don't have to grovel to them. The file was probably too long. I'll break it up and resend it."

"I searched all over for you," he said. It turned out that he learned fairly quickly from the doctor that I had gone to smoke a cigar, and he had suspected I was back at the fantail. But my father, bold adventurer, didn't want to walk back there—he might have to step over a cable or something.

"I was gone for an hour," I repeated, "an hour." It didn't get me anywhere. Plopping into the desk chair, I silently broke up the four columns into four separate files, put them on a disk, and took them up to the radio room. Roger was apologetic for setting my dad off— apparently he'd been stomping around for half an hour looking for me, worrying people. I told him I was used to it. But I wasn't. I wasn't used to people getting that mad over trifles. Even at work, Nigel notwithstanding, I wasn't used to being yelled at. This was like being fifteen years old again. Okay, he couldn't find me. Where was his philosophy now? Where was Darwin? Why couldn't he just shrug and realize that I'd get the message when I got back? He knew none of the columns were running for days. Knew that I had built in a cushion so that if the ship couldn't transmit them, I could still FedEx. Heck, I could phone tomorrow from Bridgetown and dictate. It didn't matter at all. He knew that.

My parents couldn't let go. That had been the whole problem. The mother of a friend of mine once asked my mom if they had had a child who died, because they were so protective of us. "You've baked a good cake," I'd tell my dad when I was a teenager. "Now take it out of the oven." But that didn't happen. "You're burning the cake," I'd say, as they hovered over me. When I was seventeen, my father spent the summer working for the United Nations in Geneva, and while I tried to explore my surroundings, my parents had trouble with that. I remember going out to look for nonexistent Swiss nightlife, in my ridiculous beige three-piece suit and 1977 snap-brim hat, and noticing my entire family, two blocks behind, lurking in doorways, skulking after me, watching. Eventually I would regard that moment as sweet, but I didn't then. I certainly didn't see my father getting so upset at my going on the lam to smoke a cigar as a sign of love. It was a sign of his burning the cake, still. A sign that in his heart he suspected I might hurl myself over the rail, spontaneously, out of the same incomprehensible impulse that made me grow up and date girls and contradict him in the first place.

I went to the bridge to watch the island approach, a sour knot in my stomach, numbed by gloom. The trip felt ruined. I looked miserably at the yellow lights of Barbados. Why does my father spoil everything? I thought, wanly. He always did that: birthday parties, dinners, whatever—he always worked himself into a sulk over some stupidity. My heritage.

Dr. Richardson was on the bridge, contemplating the night. "It's exciting coming into a port on a ship," he mused, scanning the docks through his binoculars. "I imagine the old days on the liners must have been unbelievable."

I looked at the doctor as if I had never seen him before. Why isn't this guy my dad? I thought, and almost said aloud, but realized how pathetic that would sound. Still, it was an intriguing idea, particularly as the Doc happily anticipated three days of "rum and beaches." My father had initially balked at going to Barbados. "What's there?" he had said. "Just beaches . . ."

I told Dr. Richardson about the evening so far and he surprised me by, rather than commiserating, suggesting that I go down and try to make nice to my father, to patch things up. I realized he was right. What else could I do?

Back in the cabin, Dad was in his pajamas, sitting up in bed, furiously scribbling away in his journal, hot loathing frozen all over his face. Silence. I broached the subject: "I know it must have been upsetting not to . . ." I began.

"I know you're an unappreciative prick," he said.

Back on the bridge, the ship was entering the harbor, with its complex machinery all lit up like a refinery. The doctor had gone. You could see the container ships offloading their cargoes. I had my notebook in my hand, and I looked at it, dully, realizing I didn't care about watching the ship dock. I didn't want to work things out with my dad. I just wanted to go home.

The *Empire State* slowly nosed past a long concrete breakwater. The breakwater was wide—it had a two-lane road lit by amber lights. Two men, tiny specks at first, sat by a white van, waiting to receive the ship's lines. There was only one tug, so the *Empire State* dropped her port anchor and carefully let out the chain as the tug pushed from the stern to increase control as the ship moved toward the pier. "There are three speeds for docking a ship," said Captain Ahlstrom, "slow, slower, and slowest."

At 10:18 P.M. the pilot boat brought the first line ashore. The men caught the rope and wrapped it around a loggerhead. As the thick manila rope went taut, the water wrung out, splattering against the mottled concrete. At 10:40 P.M., the captain called "Stop engines." I waited until I was certain my father would be asleep before returning to the room.

The next morning I awoke steamed and lay quietly in bed, listening to my father move about the cabin. Drawers were opened and shut—too many, I thought, for dressing. I wondered if he could be leaving. A long zipper would seal it—and then what would I do?

But there was no zipper, and I realized that leaving wasn't his way. Too dynamic. His way was to ignore anything that went awry and deny it if the subject came up. *What? An argument? Harsh words? Maybe to you—you're always so negative—but me, hey baby, I'm fine, positive, upbeat, thinking about higher things. Ideas. I don't know why you would feel that way, Neil. Maybe it's the drugs in high school. . . .*

I waited until he left, then showered, dressed, and stepped outside. A perfect day. Black and white swallow-tailed birds winged across a clear blue sky on the starboard side, where a cadet in whites and an officer's cap stood at parade rest at the bottom of the gangway.

I felt a bowling ball in my lungs: I wanted to go down the gangway and head to the airport. Forcing myself to sit with my father at breakfast, I squeezed a big, fake smile in his direction as I sat down. He spoke with John Perry and Gus Emig, firing some volley in my direction about how his son was worried about the safety of walking around Barbados, but he knew it would be fine. The kibitzer, coming out in moments of duress. I let him. Eventually, I patted him on the arm and said, "Let's hit town."

Cheap dockage is essential to a state school, and the *Empire State* was berthed as far down the pier as possible without still being out at sea. It took a good ten minutes to walk to the base of the pier, where there was a mall—a spacious, modern, coral-and-turquoise terminal designed to sell merchandise to cruise-ship hordes. Over the door, an enormous Cockspur rum rooster welcomed us to Barbados.

We carefully negotiated the fare for the comically brief cab ride to Trafalgar Square, the heart of Bridgetown. The sidewalks were crowded with people in polyester pants and neckties, civilization's gift to the tropics. It was Friday, a workday, and after scanning the crowd for ten seconds, I realized how ridiculous it was to have been worried about a place like this—hard-working people, going about their business.

The cab let us off. Dad was in his go mode. When I stopped to take a picture he kept walking, and I would let him disappear around the corner, then realize he was alone and double back. No matter how many times I did this, he never became aware of what I was doing and never slowed down to notice things himself.

We found the post office and Dad mailed a postcard to his brother

Morty, subtly tweaking him: "I missed you at dockside in the Bronx. We'll be in Barbados for four days and then it's on to Naples. Hope all is well. Regards to everyone. Bob."

Next we searched for the old synagogue. Unlike many sailors, my dad finds, rather than loses, religion in a foreign port. We stopped by St. Mary's Church, surrounded by a large cemetery of old graves and exotic, twisted trees. Inside the ceiling was sky blue, the church simple and quiet, just opened for the day. The caretaker gave us directions to the synagogue and handed us a pair of postcards showing the church's lovely wooden sanctuary. "This is what you be seeing there," he said in a lilt.

We set out through narrow, poorer quarters, Dad stopping to ask directions at every block even though I had a map and knew where we were going. When we got to the street, he at first refused to go down the tiny, alleylike Synagogue Lane. He waited at the intersection while I reconnoitered. "Come on, Dad!" I said, spying what had to be the place.

The graveyard was a jumble of centuries-old and modern headstones. As tradition demanded, visitors set pebbles on the gravestones to show they had been there. The graves were flat rectangles, some black with age, mottled, cratered, and broken. Parts in Hebrew, parts in the Latin of the oppressor who had forced them abroad in the first place. *"Da divina gloria."* One grave was for the infant sons of Mozley Elkin—Isaac, Joseph, David, Lindo, and Benjamin. I put a pebble on it. There was a wrecked older building, which I at first assumed was the synagogue, and a quaint little rounded pink building that turned out to be the restored old synagogue. A man appeared and opened the synagogue, explaining that the wrecked building had been a school. The synagogue was quite pretty inside—yellow walls, intricate brass chandelier, polished wood benches with delicately turned rods supporting the back. Workers had recently gut-rehabbed the entire place.

It was quiet except for the heartbeat ticking of the antique English clock.

After the synagogue visit I tried to steer us to a local restaurant for lunch, but my father wouldn't have it. We needed to go to a hotel. Whatever, I thought, images of generic Sheratons welling up in my head. We climbed into a cab and headed to the Grand Barbados Beach Club.

That turned out to be a good call. The sight of beach was instant comfort. The ocean, the same aquamarine as in the heart of the wake rolling off the bow of the *Empire State*. Guys from Maritime were renting jet skis. I took off my shoes and walked barefoot in the surf, which felt like a bath. I reached down with my fingers to taste the saltiness of the ocean.

Dad went off to find a phone and call mom. It was 11 A.M. I told him I'd wait for him in the restaurant, a comfortable, outdoor place right on the beach. I was the first customer there, and they said they weren't serving lunch.

"Are you serving beer?" I asked, sliding onto a stool at the bar.

The local brew, Banks beer, came in a sleek brown bottle tapered evenly from lip to girth. They served it very cold, and it had an ample taste. The words on the bottle, "Brewery fresh" and "Award-winning quality" seemed freighted with significance. I slugged down the beer, admiring the small black birds hopping around the bar, sticking their beaks into stacks of cups and saucers cleared away from breakfast. The counter was a Cream of Wheat color, with black-and-red specks, and I contemplated it, happily. The air smelled smoky—they were preparing barbecue for lunch.

Dad took a long time. When he showed up I was on my second Banks and engaged in a discussion with the bartender about the people pictured on each denomination of the Barbadian currency. Travelers have an automatic suspicion of the locals wherever they go. It was with relief and a bit of shame that I noticed how casually the bartender pulled out the colorful bills—reds, blues, greens—from his own wad and slapped them on the bar in front of me to illustrate the various portraits. I was charmed that the $5 bill showed Frank Worrell, a cricketer.

"It's as if we put Ernie Banks on the five back home," I said, wishing we had.

Dad wouldn't drink a beer, so he sipped an orange juice while I had two more. Heck, I thought, I'm not operating farm machinery.

The beer helped. Everyone in a book who takes a drink nowadays must, inevitably, end up facedown in the gutter, their life in ruins, or on the road to recovery, fidgeting on a metal folding chair in a church basement somewhere. Maybe that's ahead for me. But the highlight in Barbados came that hour before noon, drinking four very cold Banks beers. My father and I began to speak enthusiastically about my prospects for the future. Things were looking up. No matter its limitations, this trip sure beat being at the office. The ocean spread around us like a comforting blue blanket, warm and secure. The unpleasantness of the day before was buried. Life seemed to stretch open, and we speculated on the possibilities of success, of wealth.

"If I had a lot of money, I'd get a condo . . ." my father began, and I smiled, sitting up straight, anticipating the compliment. He'd of course want to set himself up in Chicago, close to his sons and grandchildren. ". . . in Santa Barbara and study evolutionary psychology," he continued.

Oh. I pulled silently at the Banks, deflating. Beer can't fix everything.

CHAPTER 4

Trapped Inside Some House

The engineers were obviously unhappy with the choice of Barbados, 17 degrees north of the equator. The warm water put a
strain on the ship's systems. The chief engineer kept saying, "They
moved the island"—shorthand, I believe, for "the captain should have
known better than to take this old ship this far south."

But south was our goal. The year before, the *Empire State* had
crossed the Arctic Circle, earning the cadets the "Order of the Blue
Nose," a distinction of some sort among mariners. The cadets had
marked the occasion by painting themselves blue and holding a day-
long celebration. Now Captain Ahlstrom was keen on slipping across
the equator to earn his crew an equivalent southern honor: the "Order
of the Shell Head." It seemed important to him.

The next three days in Barbados were basically a repeat of the first
day, with decreasing satisfaction. I couldn't persuade my father to explore the island. It was hard enough to get him off the ship.

Each morning I phoned Edie from the coral mall, in a large room with purple carpeting on the floor and walls, lined with thirty-two pay phones, fiercely air-conditioned, and always populated with cadets. Before leaving Chicago I had made a videotape of myself reading bedtime stories and singing lullabies to the boys, and Edie told me that not only did they watch the tape every night but they also talked to it. Before going to bed, Ross said, "Night, Daddy. I miss you. I love you" to the TV, certainly a telling comment on the cusp of the twenty-first century. Edie stressed that they missed me but were doing okay, though she kept me on the phone a long time. When I pointed out that the call was costing $2.50 a minute, and maybe I should go, she brushed off the idea. I liked that.

Seeking what novelty we could, I directed my father to a different spot called Rockly Beach, and we walked along a deserted section. The water was a lovely, undulating green, quite different from the surf at Grand Barbados. But Dad didn't seem to like there being so few people around. He was in his security mode, which could astonish me. He demurred, for instance, at my suggestion that we sit under a palm tree, concerned over the possibility of falling coconuts. So we sat a little bit away, in safety.

We tried another place farther up the beach. I felt boredom creeping in. I gazed at the white plastic chairs and the rich blue cotton pyramid umbrellas with a sort of gathering existential dread. My father talked and talked, his words peppered with a smattering of anachronistic 1960s–isms, drifting away in the warm air. Every so often I'd tune in. "It's a downer, a loser all the way . . ." he said. Then I'd drift out again.

He was describing the pleasure he got from writing down his thoughts. "I found myself sitting back, breathing deep and saying, 'My, I've got to see if I could put this down in words.' I found myself feeling good about it; it was a high I never experienced before. There was no downer associated with it, until I went to you." He noticed my expression. "Just kidding. The pleasure of writing was the high involved for me. I didn't have any visions of grandeur, of course; it wasn't as if I was the greatest writer in the world, another Hemingway. I'm like everyone else. Of course I want them to say, 'My God, Bob Steinberg's work is fantastic!' I know chances are extremely slight. I'm writing about this because I know this. I have the experience of this, and that was the pleasure, that was the high."

I suppose I should have felt happy that my dad was discovering the joy of words. But I didn't. I felt testy and annoyed. For me, writing is a struggle—one that I willingly take on, but still hard work laden with setback and doubt and disappointment. For him to sit there and giddily yabber about the fun of it seemed idiotic, like a child oohing over the distant fires of a burning city.

Dad called home. Mom was depressed; he had heard it in her voice. "She said she even misses my complaining," he said, adding that he had encouraged her to write about her feelings—it would make her feel better and lead to good prose. This surprised me, a sincere expression I couldn't easily dismiss or diminish.

The third day we asked the cabbie to take us to a fish place downtown, but he said it was closed on Sunday and steered us to the Pebbles Beach Bar & Restaurant, which turned out to be right next door to the Grand Barbados Beach Club. Just couldn't keep away from the place. Pebbles was a small bar surrounded by tables, separated from the beach by a low cinder-block wall and a metal roof. "Home of the Affordable Daiquiri" read the slogan on the menu.

They served up a very good meal of flying fish, rice, corn, plantains, vegetables, and rum punch. The punch was served with a solitary cube of ice—Barbados once was a British colony—and I asked for a cupful of ice.

Dad explained that he hadn't wanted to go on the trip because "every day is precious with Mom—we're a team." Apparently these six weeks with me were snatching those cherished days away. His father died at sixty; now he was sixty-six. I was unmoved. He had been awaiting death for the past twenty years, with the impatience of a passenger at a bus stop peering down the road. I saw it as a cheap plea for sympathy.

We watched a father, mother, and small son play cricket on the beach. The mom stood catching, behind the wicket. The dad pretended he was going to do one of those running cricket throws, then laughed and gently lobbed the ball to the little boy, who hit it quite well with a flat frat paddle. The boy tapped the bat, expectantly, waiting for the next pitch. Black chickens pecked around our table, and I flicked pieces of rice off my plate onto the red tile floor. By the fourth rum punch it occurred to me that I was overlooking the pristine birthplace of all the aqua in the world—the color that was so industrial and forlorn on grimy hospital corridor walls looked perfect here, climbing up onto the beach as surf.

"Well, tomorrow at this time . . ." said my father, parodying his tendency to plan ahead, "we'll be here." And we both laughed big laughs.

Next morning, the bridge was empty at 7 A.M., since the ship was docked. There was a warning posted: someone had tripped the Global Maritime Distress and Safety System alarm the night before, and the *Empire State* had managed the dubious feat of sending an S.O.S. to every ship on earth while tied up snugly at the pier in Bridgetown. My father, the former radio operator, took immense satisfaction in this, and I must admit that I did, too.

All was quiet. Within the break wall, the water was a shimmering molasses except where sun inscribed itself into it, a streak of burning yellow with an aura of blue, as if blasting the true color out of the dirty harbor. There was a smoky tang in the air.

Returning to the cabin, I resolved to interest my father in doing something beside the beach—three days was enough. The ship didn't sail until 5 P.M. There was a botanical garden on the other side of the island. We could rent a car. There was the Mount Gay rum factory tour. Or a cigar-rolling factory; the doctor had gone there and liked it.

"The doctor is an interesting guy," my dad mused. "He takes it easy, looks around, makes the best of wherever he's at."

A lesson for us all, I thought. I might as well have said it. Dad wouldn't go to the factory. He wouldn't go on the tour. He certainly wouldn't go to the botanical garden. "The gardens are the wrong place to wander around," he said.

In his defense, I did not insist. I did not grab him by the earlobe and drag him away, saying, "We're going." I tried a few times, shrugged, and gave up, thinking, *At least there's drinks.*

We went back, yet again, to the Grand Barbados Beach Club. We walked on the beach, briefly, and by 11 A.M. were at the bar, drinking rum punches. The good feeling of the first day wasn't there, however, and we went back to Pebbles. The waitress remembered that I took a lot of ice, which flattered me. A regular. We had a good lunch and though we started with one of my father's pet topics—a critique of the mind, based on Darwinism—we gradually slid, fueled perhaps by the rum punches, into the heart of the matter between us.

I always faulted my parents for preferring to hang out at the Boulder retiree scene when my brother and I were in Chicago with our families. It seemed to me both selfish and unwise.

"Let me tell you something, Neil," my father said. "I don't see you as the type to hover around your grandchildren, either. Doesn't mean you're not there for them. But not sitting and waiting."

My father's central concept—perhaps his only concept—of being a grandparent was the memory of his grandmother Bertha perched at her apartment window in the Bronx, wringing her hands and waiting for someone to come by.

"That 'sitting and waiting' image is a tough one," I said. "You say that a lot, 'sitting and waiting.' Mom's sitting and waiting for friends who aren't calling her."

Dad was upset that, despite being gone for six weeks, my mother's coterie of friends in Colorado had not rallied to occupy her time.

True, her closest friends were themselves busy having operations and attending to emergencies in their own lives. But it still felt like abandonment.

"The world isn't perfect," he said. "You take what you can get. But to my way of thinking, for me to sit at that home at the end of your street, for me to sit there and wait for my grandchildren to wave to me from the ground floor, forget about it. Look—ideally, you live in the area you grew up in, your family lives there, your relatives live there, children come over and say, 'Grandpa, tell me how it was.' "

"You're involved," I said.

"You're involved," my father allowed. "You talk to them. They're part of your life. That's a world that existed in New York City a hundred years ago."

"It exists in Skokie," I said. My in-laws live in Skokie, surrounded by their children and grandchildren. I was so unaccustomed to a tight-knit family that, for the first few years I dated my wife-to-be, I found her family off-putting—this large clan of people who hung out together. It was strange. Only as the years passed did I realize a family was something good to have.

"Maybe it exists in Skokie," he said. "But I'll tell you something; it doesn't exist in most places. It's the truth. Kids move out, they go somewhere else, their jobs take them to somewhere else. And people travel to be with them. It's not the best of both possible worlds. There's no question about it. It's a compromise and it may turn out to be a bummer."

"I'll tell you my view, and we'll see if I'm going to be wrong," I said. "You guys will be there until old age grabs you by the throat and gives a few shakes, then you'll say, 'Hell, we need our kids around us,' and you'll show up with your demands, and say, 'How come you're not seeing us all the time? How come you're not paying us our due?' To the last moment, you'll be out there doing your thing, then you'll show up and say, 'What kind of ingrates are you? Take care of us!' It would have been nice if you could have shown up a few years early and put some money in the bank."

"I think you have an erroneous, crass view of things," my father said.

"It may be crass but it's true," I said.

"You have a view that disturbs me," he said. "It's the view of a person who balances things by 'what-I-get-and-what-I-give.' "

"That's how life is, isn't it?" I said.

"Uh-uh, no way, no way," he said. "You as a parent will find out— you're finding out right now. You talk about them in loving terms, which you should as a father. But I can tell you right now we talked about our kids in those same loving ways."

"That's what worries me," I said. "I'm sure you did."

"We wanted to give our kids the best and we did. We really did. They're off on their own now—they've made their choice of mates. They go off on their own and they do their things. We like to be around them, but we do not want to be in Chicago, as simple as that. We simply do not want to be in Chicago. If you do not want to be in Chicago, there's no choice, you don't go there in the first place. If we did, we'd be sitting there waiting. I love Chicago—the people are wonderful. The thing I don't love about it is the fucking weather. It's terrible as far as I'm concerned, especially as you get older. You haven't been older. I admire your in-laws. They're lucky. They're fortunate, no question about it. I'm saying for most people, they don't have that; they go where they can spend their years where they can enjoy themselves. Every time we come to Chicago we spend a thousand bucks seeing you guys. We love it. We don't bitch about it. We love it. We think it's wonderful. But to sit there and wait to be a part of the family. Mom wants it more than I. . . ."

"To live your lives *integrated* with your family," I said. "As for sitting there, waiting: if Sam doesn't call Mom on the phone, after a while she is upset about it."

"She should be."

"Because she's sitting there and waiting for him to call, only she's a thousand miles away. If she lived in Arlington Heights, she could go over there and bring cookies."

"Let me tell you something," my father said, getting down to brass tacks. "To take another subject. As far as Sam goes, he's strange, no matter what. If you lived next door to him—*ze gournish helfin* as far as I'm concerned." My father rarely lapses into Yiddish, except under duress, such as spitting out the term for "it wouldn't help."

Dad felt we should just be happy that they are happy, wherever they are.

"I have met children who don't have your point of view," he said. "Children who say, 'My parents, no matter what. Whatever is good for them, it's about time, it's about time they did something for themselves instead of always giving to us. Let them do what they want.' I don't get that from you. I get. . . ." And here he mimicked a high, whining voice. " 'Hey, Dad, when you're eighty, you'll need your diaper changed, you'll show up here, man, don't expect anything from me.' That's what you told me. That's crass crap."

He was right, halfway. I had used the diaper image—which had burned into his mind. But my point was entirely missed.

"The 'don't expect anything from me' is your own lineage talking, Dad," I said. "The fact is, I'm going to have to do whatever is necessary."

That was the real reason I wanted them in Chicago. Not that I really thought they'd be a pleasant, regular part of life. Frankly, I couldn't imagine that. I didn't think he was capable. There was one moment when my father had killed that dream in one smooth stroke. They were visiting us in Chicago, staying at a posh downtown hotel. The plan was for us to rendezvous at the Children's Museum at Navy Pier. I showed up with Ross, age two, at the zenith of angel-faced cuteness. My parents arrived. We went to enter the museum. Admission was $6 a person. My father pulled back. "Why don't I wait for you in the bookstore?" he said. "Dad," I said, "we're going in the museum. You're visiting your two-year-old grandson. This is your one chance." I made him spend the six bucks and go in, but he sulked the whole time, and I couldn't help but look at him, scowling in the corner while Ross innocently played, and think, *You idiot.* The experience carbonized my brain.

So it wasn't that I expected him to teach my boys to fish; heck, he hadn't taught *me* to fish. My motivation was glimpsing into the murk of the future and seeing them, faces tight with age and confusion, arms clasped across themselves, arriving at the last possible moment, these sinkholes of need, spreading their demands before us like peddlers setting out wares on a blanket. I'd have to buy, have to do whatever was necessary—I owed them that for bringing me into the world and raising me, if not to whistling happiness, then at least to a certain functionability. I would have rather done it gladly, earnestly, with the sense of leaping duty and love I feel toward my in-laws. But that wasn't their way and never would be. My father didn't get it at all.

"For my parents, I would have done anything," he said. "Even my father. I couldn't stand his guts half the time. It didn't matter; I was his son. I would do anything. I was concerned about him because he was my father. And I wanted the best for him."

"That's why I'm concerned about you," I said. "Don't you think it's best for you to come to Chicago?"

"I do not," he said.

The sticking point was that we viewed the same event—his being a father—in two completely opposite ways. To him, he was a fountain of generosity, constantly giving. Selfish people always feel that way. I saw him as distant and self-absorbed, El Numero Uno in his own eyes, busy attending to his own needs, someone who never gave aid, material or emotional, that he could find a way to withhold. This didn't leave us much middle ground, and the conversation swung onto a subject that illustrated this all too perfectly, to my boggled horror.

For instance, this trip, he said. Sacrifice, on his part, on my behalf. A selfless act, agreeing to go on the ship.

"I almost didn't come because of what an asshole you were in Colorado in March," he said. "It took two days for Mom to talk me out of it, for her to convince me to come."

I was stunned. Three months before the cruise, Edie and I and the boys went to visit my parents in Colorado, to put in face time with my father and make sure his resolve was steeled. What had I done? I wanted to know. Hadn't I taken my two children in diapers on a plane to see him, rented a car? What?

"The Chinese food," he said. "Any other child would have said, 'Whatever you want, Mom.' Why couldn't you show her that respect?"

I slipped from stunned to appalled. My parents of course lost interest in my boys about fifteen minutes after they arrived, and spent the next four days guarding their possessions and looking forward to our leaving. On the last night, when my wife was upstairs giving Kent his bottle, my mother announced that she would be ordering Chinese food and was there anything I wanted.

"Edie will be finished in a minute," I said. "Can we wait and ask her what she'd like?"

No, my mother said, it takes an hour to get the food. She was hungry. "Five minutes, Ma," I said. "What's the big deal?" We went back and forth for a while, until I said, "Here's an idea: why don't Edie and I go out for dinner, then you can order whatever the fuck you want?"

Needless to say, that put a pall over the proceedings, particularly since we left the next day and there wasn't enough time to cultivate jollity. The anger lingered with me. After I returned to Chicago, I was still shaking my head and muttering, riding the 151 bus to the

Wrigley Building. It took a half hour of ranting to Sam until I finally calmed down.

And now, as the final, crowning ignominy, my father thought it was *me* misbehaving, and had been holding it against me for months. He was ready to chuck the trip because I had asked my mother to hold off ordering dinner until Edie came downstairs.

Impatient for the waitress, I headed to the bar for the next rum punch.

Not only was he willing to chuck the trip back in March, he said, but he was poised to leave in Charleston as well, and Mom—whom I had been worried about talking him into going home—had to struggle to convince him not to.

Eventually we talked ourselves out. We sat there, the music wafting over us. I looked at the sea, the sandy beach, the bright ships at anchor, the purple posts of the bar. The lovely scene somehow enhanced my feeling of misery. We both felt that way. We halfheartedly joked about going to the airport—I'm sure if I slapped my palm on the table, and said, "Let's do it," he would have.

But we didn't. We went back to the ship, stopping at a food market to pick up a bottle of Cockspur on the way. I didn't tell him that I had already picked up a bottle on my own the first day. I wanted it to be a surprise reserve.

I felt very bad when I returned. A sort of suffocated, grief-stricken feeling. The shock of the return of the Chinese food, and the way my father neatly erased any credit I might give him for going on the trip by casting it as yet another sacrifice, and a grudging sacrifice at that, something he had to be talked into by my mother—twice. It just blew me away. I was destroyed, though when I saw my father's long face in our cabin I fought to rally ourselves.

"Are you ready to sail the Atlantic?" I asked, a false note of cheeriness in my voice.

"Does it matter?" he said, morosely.

There was a long silence, and I was just about beginning to brood on his not asking me whether I was ready when he surprised me by doing just that. I thought about the question for a second, genuinely uncertain. "Yes," I lied. "I think I am. We had fun in Barbados."

There was a knock on the door. Colin, my freckled, Huck Finn cadet. The gang wanted to be taught a previous class that none of them showed up for. In half an hour. My Dad, standing behind Colin, shook his head emphatically, *No*.

Thanks, Dad, I thought, *I'm thirty-eight years old. I'll handle this.* I stepped out into the hall and assessed my options. In my heart, I didn't want to teach right away: 5:30 P.M.—the ship was supposed to leave to sail the Atlantic at 7 P.M. Obviously a moment of high drama. If I were teaching, I'd miss the departure.

But after tonight, the cadets had watch for two days. If I wanted my students to move forward I needed to get the classwork out of the way whenever I could. I said okay.

Grabbing my materials, I headed belowdecks. I felt sick, sitting in the hot, windowless C1 classroom. With ninety minutes before the lines were to be cast off, it occurred to me that my father had been a monster far away. A beast on Pluto. And I, in my foolishness, invited him to depart Pluto and live with me, for this endless stretch of time. Forty-two days. Only eighteen had passed; twenty-four more to go, the next fourteen on the high seas in a little cabin.

There was a note on the blackboard from five students—all female—who "were told" class was at 5 P.M. Not by me, I thought, erasing it. It was after 5:30 P.M.

My face was numb with upset: no students, no chance of coming to terms with my father. That damn Chinese food. So peevish and small and mean. What got to me was that my father was ready to revise his entire opinion of me, assuming that he didn't think I was an asshole all the time, which might be a big assumption, and scuttle the trip—all based on my asking my mother to wait a few minutes for my wife before ordering dinner. Hadn't I built up any reserve of goodwill at all? Obviously not.

Some students showed up. I taught the class. Walking back through the ship to the bridge, I struggled to think my way out of the box. My father was right. It did boil down to respect. Dad wanted blanket respect—obeisance, even. Why not just say, "Mom, order whatever you like"? Because I wanted Edie to be considered. Because my wife might find it rude that her feelings didn't matter. Perhaps I should cultivate insincerity, be more of a go-between—kiss up to my parents in a believable fashion that they would consider respect but would actually be lack of respect bordering on fear; the head-nodding, backing-away, palms out, fingers-spread placation you'd give a crazy person. "Yes, yes, Mom, of course, you order your Chinese food *right away.* I'm sure Edie and I will love whatever you select." Then run to Edie and roll my eyes and shrug and whisper that I tried to stop my mother from ordering, but the big feed bell in her head had gone off and she could not be resisted and I'm very sorry. Is that what they want? That's probably what most adult children do. How angry could Edie be? She sure wouldn't be talking about it three months later.

On the bridge I watched a sugarcane ship, the *Paxi,* leave ahead of us. "The last time I left here I was on a sugar ship," mused the captain, watching the *Paxi,* about our length but twice the weight, move slowly out of the harbor with a load of cane.

We were about to sail the Atlantic Ocean. I felt nothing but stress. Another highlight blown. I tried to spark a flash of excitement: this should be thrilling; I ought to be thrilled. I owed it to the child I had once been. I owed it to Robert Louis Stevenson: "And steps coming down in an orderly way / To where my toy vessels lie safe in the bay / This one is sailing and that one is moored / Hark to the song of the sailors on board!"

Dad appeared on the starboard bridge. I went over and rubbed his back. "I'm glad you're not in your stateroom packing," I said. "My bags are on the dock," he joked, in a flat voice.

"We're going to have fun," I said. No reply.

I tried again. "So you're going to cross the Atlantic; how do you feel?" I asked.

"I want to get on with it," he said. "When the ship left Fort Schuyler, that's when I felt it was in the Atlantic. This is a diversion, Barbados. I'm expecting a reasonably good crossing."

The sun was setting; the water a deep teal. I looked over at the breakwater. The gangway was still down. I had a brief moment of imagining running to the room, throwing everything into the suitcase, clattering down the steps. Not that I was considering it, but I was trying to pry back a corner of the bolted door of my resolve and peek through the space, feeling a trace of the anxiety that such an act would produce—the scrambling panic, my father yelling at me, quickly packing himself, not wanting to be left on the ship, alone.

Then I let the door slam shut. If you are loose in your resolve, then your decisions torture you as events risk shattering them. I looked up, breathed the air. I was going to sea with my father. I was going to cross the Atlantic for two weeks. We were going to Italy. I would not run gibbering home. To do that would be to doom myself.

That was Lord Jim's mistake—a moment's cowardice, abandoning the *Padua* and its eight hundred sleeping pilgrims at what he thought was the approach of disaster. He spent the rest of his life trying to escape the shame, which followed him across the world like a faithful dog.

Always a bad idea, to give up the ship. I remembered Commander Oliver Hazard Perry, a hero of mine. His battle flag proclaimed: "Don't Give Up the Ship." Do not quit, if you can help it. Hang on when things get rough.

As corny as it sounds, I derived strength from remembering the failure of Lord Jim and the success of Perry. I had blown the first two weeks, forgetting what I was trying to do and falling into old, destructive routines. But there was still time. I could salvage the trip. I would fix things. People don't change—I still believed that—but now I wanted to. I could build something new with my father. Or at least understand what had happened to him, why he was the way he was. I had to. I would not be put off by his manner, his exterior, his thorny defenses. I would brave the thicket and bring back his story, his real story.

There is a reality, after all, isn't there, lurking at the bottom of our quirks and opinions and perceptions? A bedrock of truth. We had only begun to talk about the past. I had tried to sit my dad down every morning and interview him. It was tough, because we always circled back to the same swamp of bad feelings—toward his father, his brother, his family. It was so grim that I was usually good for about thirty minutes and then I had to give up for the day and do something else, waiting for the gloom to disperse. Still, I kept at it, prodding, trying to glimpse the true outlines of his life through the fog of decades.

Just before the *Empire State* departed, there was a moment of calm. Everything seemed motionless, stationary, like a model-train diorama. The figures on the breakwater, the tug—all waiting in the quietness of a beginning. I stood at the starboard rail, looking at a flashing red light at the end of the pier and, beyond it, a green buoy light, flashing as if in reply. The water lapped. Somewhere, a mechanical humming. At 7 P.M. the captain ordered, "Let go aft lines," and the voyage was under way. A star appeared in the deep blue sky and I wished upon it.

The *Empire State* steamed off into the night. I stayed on the bridge wing, watching Barbados and its lights recede, disappearing over the horizon as the ship headed into the vast blackness of the ocean. Suddenly I felt genuinely afraid: a tiny man on a little ship of humanity entering an immense, frightening darkness.

Seaward was pitch black. My eyes strained into the inky void, searching for the comfort of a horizon. Instead, the past, like a great sea monster, reared up out of the ocean before me.

BOOK TWO

Going Nowhere

Save your time and trouble
Save your railroad fare
'Cause when you leave New York
You don't go anywhere.

—GORDON JENKINS

Bobby thinks of himself as a corvette. This is before the sports car, when corvettes are still sleek, fast, lightly armed military ships. The people in the street are ships, too, but bigger ships, slower ships. A fat guy walking his cigar might be a battleship; a lady with a brace of dogs, a convoy; an older boy, a destroyer. Bobby races past them all, full steam ahead, legs pumping, snaking a path through the crowded sidewalk, fast, unseen. Maybe someone is chasing him. Maybe he's late for school. Maybe he's just running because he can't stand to wait behind all those weightier vessels, moving so slowly they are practically bobbing at anchor.

He dreams of shoes with wheels. Hidden flat in the soles, wheels that would snap down at the click of a secret button and then—whoosh!—away he'd skate. That would give those Italian kids something to think about.

CHAPTER 5

How Can We Get to the Ocean? — The Bronx, 1940

Bobby is a lucky boy. His mother is a wonderful cook—briskets and casseroles and oval platters piled with scrambled eggs. "This is delicious, Ma," he says, digging in. "Delicious."

He goes to the World's Fair and sees the Talking Robot and the World of Tomorrow with all its little cars. His uncle, who works at the fair, slips him a real Heinz pickle pin, just like the one worn by the official fair employees. Bobby sees Roosevelt go down Third Avenue. He and his father, Sam, take a break from the sign-painting shop to stand at the curb at the corner of 149th Street. They wait with the crowd. At the first sight of the motorcycle outriders, his father boosts him up on his shoulders and Bobby glimpses Roosevelt, or his top hat anyway, as the big open car flies by.

The war comes. Bobby is in his Aunt Jeanne's yellow kitchen that famous Sunday. Her husband, a radio repairman, is showing Bobby the latest model—a receiver with a tuning eye that glows red when you lock onto a station. Fantastic. They are sitting at the small square metal table, twiddling from one station to the next, watching the eye go on then off, when they hear it. "We interrupt this program to bring you a special news bulletin. . . ."

The next day, Monday, the principal at P.S. 105, the imperial Nellie L. R. Goodwin, gathers the students on the playground. It is war, she says gravely, and they all must do their share. And they do. Bobby's mother teaches him to knit, and he knits squares that will turn into blankets for soldiers. Later, in junior high, he carves small planes from pinewood blocks. Mr. Walsh hands them out at school as kits: the block, the templates, the blue prints. Bobby paints them black and gives them to the school to turn over to the U.S. Navy for use in gunnery identification training. You have to get it just right—the exact outline of the tail, the exact angle of the wing's dihedral, following a template—or otherwise they're no good and the Navy will reject them. Bobby gets it exactly right, and puts himself to sleep at night imagining that somewhere, on some atoll in the Pacific, there's a Marine in a dug-out anti-aircraft gun emplacement, surrounded by sandbags and covered with camouflage net, squinting at specks high in the sky, gazing, gazing, gazing, then freezing, only for a second, before throwing back the netting, hopping into the chair, spinning the handles, swinging his gun up and around, peering through the gunsight, then opening fire, the twin barrels erupting, reciprocating back and forth, steam rising off the barrels, hot shells flipping overhead and clattering to the dirt, the tracers *screaming* out into the sky. The Zero—or Ki-22, or Aichi "Val" dive bomber, depending on Bobby's whim that evening—breaks apart overhead, the pieces pinwheeling to earth. All because of the pinewood models Bobby Steinberg carves in his bedroom in the Bronx.

It gets better. They're assembling gliders for the Army in an old bus garage on Kingsbridge Road, and his father is hired to do the lettering—CAUTION: TOW RELEASE—and to paint the big Army star on the side. All day Saturday, Bobby stands in the doorways of those glider bodies, lined up in the dim, cavernous garage, and sees the French landscape rolling under him. Sometimes Italy. His hands grip the imaginary parachute, like a khaki belly. He goes through the motions of hooking up his line and waiting in the door for the signal, knees slightly bent. "Go! Go! Go!" He hops out the door, falls a foot to the garage floor, lands, rolls, then springs up again, gathering the billows of his imaginary parachute before the Jerries see it. His father, steadying his sable brush against the long pole, knobbed at each end, that painters have used for a thousand years, doesn't look up.

The war is over and won. On V-J Day, Bobby, age thirteen, huddles by his bedroom window, sitting on the cold radiator cover with the three-crystal radio he built himself, listening through an earpiece to descriptions of the chaotic joy in the streets. He doesn't bother going outdoors to look himself—why, when he has the whole world brought right there and set before him on his homemade plywood desk? "We take you now to Honolulu, Hawaii. Hello, Honolulu?"

Not that every day is V-J Day. As Bobby gets older, the good times give way to trouble. His father, Sam—a man you tiptoe around. Trouble. The sign shop on 149th Street, across from St. Mary's Park, where the winos hang out. Trouble. Every Saturday morning and all summer long: "Paint an eagle here, Bobby!" "Bobby, take this over to the Chesterfield Arms, 124 West 140th Street." "Bobby, answer the phone!" As if he were a slave.

Trouble. His brother Morty—never a time when there wasn't a shroud of irony around that term: "my brother." Three years older than Bobby. Fists like rocks. Once, Bobby is following Morty and two of his friends down the street; the group stops and the pair of friends—big lunks like Morty—backtrack to Bobby and beat him up, while Morty, hands in pockets, at a discreet distance, carefully examines the sky, rocking on his heels and whistling.

All right, maybe Bobby brings some of that trouble on himself.

There is the time when Bobby falls out of bed and starts crying. His father bursts in, in his strap t-shirt and boxer shorts. Half-asleep, Bobby cries out, "Morty did it!" and Sam takes a belt to Morty, who is completely asleep.

Trouble. Morty's bicycle—a cream and white Schwinn. The bar mitzvah bicycle. Bobby shouldn't have ridden it. But Bobby doesn't have a bicycle, and Morty carelessly runs the lock through the bicycle chain and nothing else, as if he doesn't really care if somebody rides it or not. Bobby senses an opportunity: the lock chain could be suspended, carefully, with strings, so that the bike chain passes through the lock chain, undisturbed. Who knew he'd ride right by Morty and his pals? Who knew that a bunch of guys could outrun a bike?

So, trouble from without and trouble he brings on himself.

Trouble. The synagogue. Two blocks down Pelham Parkway, a massive, fortlike building, filled with bearded, jabbering old men who teach Hebrew phonetically but don't bother with what the words actually mean. Scary old men. The stern, hand-cracking routine that worked so well in the *shtetl* in Europe doesn't work at all in the Bronx, where the American kids just laugh and run off. The old men are raising a generation of disbelievers and don't even know it, don't even sense the religion sizzling away, like steam, all around them—steam from the tears of the Old World hitting the frying pan of the New.

Still, Bobby goes there to say prayers in the morning, to put on prayer boxes and utter words he doesn't understand to a God he doesn't believe in, simply because it allows him to be twenty minutes late for school every single day and have a signed excuse.

Trouble. Dad and Morty, the old bearded men, and the Italian kids and *girls*, smoothing their cotton dresses over their knees. What is it about girls? Nobody says. Nobody asks.

Trouble. Still, never trouble so bad that it doesn't fall away half a page into an Edward Ellsberg submarine book: *Submerged* or *Men Un-*

der the Sea or *Ocean Gold* or *Treasure Below* or *Thirty Fathoms Deep.*
Crack one open anywhere:

> *At 3 A.M., the doctor came out of the chamber, wan and weak. He
> said: "If we're going to save L'Heureux's life, we've got to get him to
> a hospital!" Lieutenant Hartley let go his mooring; soon the Falcon
> was making full speed toward Newport. At 7 A.M., she ran along-
> side the dock there, where an ambulance was waiting. . . .*

You'd have to be a dunce not to make the connection. Not to look up
from *On the Bottom,* distracted by some commotion in the apartment—
Sam coming home: "Hey, Moonface, how was school today? Didja kiss
your cross-eyed girlfriend?"—and think: *I could get away from this.
I could let go my mooring and be gone.* You'd have to be dead not to
think it.

Until the day Bobby ships out with Commander Ellsberg, however,
there is radio. Radio is science and excitement. A hobby and a career
all in one. It is a discipline not open to the lazy. Sure, every Boy Scout
knows Morse code. But can any of them send it at twenty words a
minute, the minimum to pass the test for your official State of New
York ham radio license? No way. That takes work.

Building a radio takes work, too, even from a Heathkit. A schematic
in one hand, a soldering iron in the other, tongue exploring the corner
of your mouth. One big tube, like a prize egg, nesting in the center of
a circuitboard. It takes hours.

A radio needs an antenna. Sure, you can run one up the wall in your
bedroom, but that's a joke. Bobby replaces a pane of glass in his bedroom window with a sheet of Plexiglas cut from scrap at the sign shop.
He drills a hole in the Plexiglas with his father's hand drill, then runs a
wire through the hole, up the outside brick wall, five floors to the roof.

How does he do it? Easy. His friend Herman goes up to the roof and lowers the wire, and Bobby snags it with a coat hanger twisted into a hook, then pulls it in. You can do anything with ingenuity and the help of a friend or two.

Lots of work. But the thrill—to connect the final wire to a pole of the big, square nine-volt battery with the leaping electric cat on it. To see the heart of the tube glow orange, and to fit the headphones over your ears, and twiddle the knob, listening, fore and middle fingers extended, poised over the key, waiting, waiting . . . catching the faint, rapid clicks—*dah dah, dit dit dit dit dah, dit dah dit, dah*—clicks you understand. "M4RT2, M4RT2. . . ." Someone's call letters. Bobby's right hand taps out, "W2DDM, W2DDM. . . ." His call letters. They converse. It turns out he is talking to a man in Allentown, Pennsylvania, or another kid in Bangor, Maine. Bangor, Maine! Can you imagine? From his bedroom on Barnes Avenue in the Bronx. Amazing.

Radio isn't all, however. There are model airplanes. By the time Bobby goes to work turning out little black models for the military, he is already an old pro.

Gliders, at first—simple generic planes quickly constructed out of sheets of balsa wood. You take them to Van Cortlandt Park to fly on the wind or with a wind-up rubber-band propeller.

That gets old fast. You can't toss a glider very long when a few feet away another boy is priming the Hornet engine on the bright red Fokker triplane he has constructed from a kit.

Soon Bobby is at it as well—not with Hornet engines, which cost a fortune, but with OK-60s, the best he can afford. He turns out planes like a factory. Famous planes. The Sopwith Camel. The Grumman Gulfhawk. The Granville Gee-Bee Super Sportster.

All it takes is $1 for a kit and a lot of time and careful effort. First, you spread the plans over a board. Then, you cover the plans with a sheet of waxed paper and pin it down. Cut the pieces out of the balsa sheets provided in the kit: struts and leading edges, ribs and curved supports. These you delicately piece together on the waxed paper, pinning each one as it is glued in place—lightly, not too much glue, the mark of an amateur.

After a few hours' assembly, and a day to dry, you remove the pins and triumphantly lift up part of the plane: a wing, a tail, a section of fuselage.

But only in skeleton, a balsa skeleton, the promise of an airplane. Then it must be covered with tissue paper—special paper that shrinks into a taut skin when you paint it with clear dope. The pieces are assembled, the plane painted, and the decals soaked in a bowl of warm water and slid carefully into place. Last, the engine is mounted on the firewall with four tiny metal screws.

Then you have a plane you can take to the park and fly on a wire and hope you don't smash all over the concrete—all that work undone by a downdraft or a slip of the wrist.

Bobby doesn't fly his airplanes much. He likes to keep the planes he builds. They hang from the ceiling of his bedroom, along with Morty's planes—they share the room—a veritable air force. What a feeling of pride, of accomplishment, just to open your eyes in the morning, to fold your hands behind your head, lingering a moment before rushing off to school, to see them, slowly wheeling around on their strings in a breeze coming through the open window to the air shaft. As if they're flying overhead, protecting you from attack.

The attack comes anyway. Sam calls Bobby "Moonface" for Moonface Mullins, the kid sleeping in a dresser drawer in the comic strip "Gasoline Alley." Bobby does have a big round face, at least until he's ten, and he does like to sleep, particularly Saturday mornings at 5 A.M., when he should be getting up to go to the sign shop. Sam calls him Moonface in front of his friends, and soon everybody does.

That's his father's way. Sam Steinberg will tell your girlfriend that she has fat ankles. He'll tell you that you are short. Without looking up from his newspaper he'll deliver a zinger that will haunt you for the rest of your life—anything to put you in your place and, by implication, elevate himself above you.

Sam will tell you that he is a "commercial artist," not a sign painter. A sign painter is some schmuck from Brooklyn freehanding chunky letters in the window of a grocery store and dripping paint on his shoes. That's not Sam. Never a sign painter. A "commercial artist." Sam studied art at Cooper Union. He arrives at a job dressed like a banker and leaves the same way.

He has illusions of grandeur. He won't tell you that, but it's plain to those around him. The big Buick—later a LaSalle, a 1936 LaSalle, shiny and flaunted, purchased at an auction from the Rockefeller estate. A Rockefeller LaSalle. Sam has style. He wears his hat at a cocky angle, sighting you along its brim like a gun. He combs a strand of hair over his bald head as long as he can, just like MacArthur.

Sam Steinberg is not cheap. People accuse him of being cheap, but he is not cheap. When it comes to himself, a man of his position, nothing is too good: Hart, Schaffner & Marx suits, Corona cigars, hats from Macy's. True, when it comes to spending money on other people, a certain tightness creeps in. Okay, rushes in and pitches a tent.

At the sign shop, he hires anybody who will work for near to nothing: a drunk ex-Marine, shattered from the war; a skeletal old man, Isadore Englehard. And of course his sons, who must paint signs to earn their allowances.

Everybody has a story. One week Sam pays his long-time assistant, Chester, a penny too much. The next day, Sam realizes his mistake and confronts Chester as he walks into the shop. He demands the penny back. "Sam, it's just a penny," Chester beseeches. Sam keeps his hand extended. "Yeah, but it's *my* penny," he says.

At age twelve, Bobby pickets his father's place. He had asked for a raise—a quarter a week is too little—and been turned down flat. So he takes two pieces of cardboard and letters, expertly, STEINBERG SIGN

COMPANY UNFAIR TO LABOR on both, and strings them together to make a sandwich sign. He doesn't picket all day, but waits until he knows his father is about to arrive, then begins marching back and forth in front of the shop.

A yank at the collar and he's back inside. His father's face, close to his. "Fifty cents," his father says. Strike over.

But money is not the real problem for Bobby. The real problem is the work, the sign shop. Breathing in those fumes. Painting arrows. "BIG SALE!" Painting numerals, backward, on the inside of glass doors. First, sketch the number in grease pencil on the front of the glass, then fill in the outline on the other side with quick-drying varnish. When it reaches a certain tackiness, when you can just put your hand on it and it feels a little damp, you paint in the number with melted isinglass. Then the gold. Take a guilder's tip and rub it in your hair to create a little static electricity, then use it to pick up the leaf, bringing it up to the glass, closer and closer, until it jumps onto the surface. The gold leaf sticks to the isinglass. You rub it off with a cotton ball elsewhere, saving the old cotton balls in a jar to sell to the goldmonger later. Then Japan Black. Then more varnish.

Try that two or three times on every door in a new sixteen-story office building. It gets old. As does heading out to New Jersey to put up a big billboard for Frigidaire. As does dragging into those Irish bars to paint a line announcing the arrival of television across the inside of the window, backward. As does standing beside his father, silently, while Sam slices pennies with the owner, those pink Mick faces looking up from their booze—the murmured insults, just out of earshot, the oscillating fan seeming to go *kike-kike-kike-kike* . . . , the compressor on the big cooler humming *hebe-hebe-hebe-hebe-hebe*. . . .

Give Sam Steinberg credit: his cheapness is not total. He sends his family away for the summer. Gets the boys out of the city heat. The Steinbergs spend a month or six weeks in the mountains, at the Lake

House, in the hills of Woodbridge, New Jersey. Morty and Bobby swim in the cold, clear water. There are trees with swings, a large dining room, a real farm across the road. Bobby's mother, Frances, is relaxed and happy, deeply tan, eating good food that she doesn't have to cook herself. Lots of other kids, fishing, playing baseball, putting on plays.

Sam drives up on the weekends. About two hours from the Bronx. He closes the shop early to get there by the end of dinner. As 7 P.M. approaches, Bobby and Morty find themselves drifting toward the road, toward the Six-Ton Bridge, as they call it, for a sign on it saying: LOAD LIMIT SIX TONS.

When Sam crosses the bridge he blows the horn three times, *beep-beep beeeeeeeep,* a triumphal blast announcing the arrival of the king. And the boys come running, waving, across the field, toward the car, for hugs and kisses and to see what gift he has brought from the city: a leather basketball, a Parcheesi board game, a new bamboo fishing pole.

Sam's brothers, Burt and Julie, are in business together—The B. Steinberg Jewelry Company. Costume jewelry. Cheap stuff. To the trade only. A factory on West 36th Street.

Bobby works there the summer he's sixteen, soldering the backs on pins. Sitting at a long assembly line, a lone white teen among a dozen Puerto Rican women, illegals, docile as slaves. Bobby once rides in the elevator with his uncle Julie and one of the Puerto Rican women.

"What do you think of these titties, Bobby?" Julie says, placing a hand on the top of the woman's breast. "Nice, huh?" Uncle Julie laughs. Bobby stares down at the floor, his face hot. The woman looks straight ahead as if nothing is happening.

That's his family. Burt is a gambler. He has an apartment near Yankee Stadium. His father says Burt bets a thousand dollars a week on the Yankees games. Bobby likes to believe that's just his dad showing off, but what if it's true? A thousand dollars!

How Can We Get to the Ocean? — The Bronx, 1940

Shameful boast or ugly fact? Who knows? That's the choice you get with Sam Steinberg. It does not inspire you to stick around. Bobby writes to the Cushman Motor Scooter Company: if they would provide him with a scooter, and transport from the Bronx to Europe, he will ride their product from city to city, promoting Cushman. Answer: no, thank-you. The Harley-Davidson Motorcycle Company? No, thank-you.

He writes to Prince Rainier, of the Republic of Monaco, after he reads that the tiny nation has no amateur radio station. If the republic covers his transportation to Monaco and his expenses there, he will set up the country's first amateur station and use it to publicize Monaco. The equipment will be donated by the National Radio Company. He also writes to National Radio in Worcester, Massachusetts: if they donate equipment for an amateur radio station, he will take it to Monaco at no cost to them and use it to promote National Radio.

No, thank-you.

In truth, by then the thrill of radio has worn off. You call out into the darkness: "W2DDM, W2DDM." You reach someone: together, you marvel at the distance between you, discuss the weather, compare equipment. The next day, you do it again with somebody else. So what?

Bobby isn't really trying to promote radio, anyway. He is trying to promote himself away from the Bronx. Maybe the companies he writes to somehow sense that in rejecting him.

Not that the Bronx is so terrible. The Bronx is nice. Barnes Avenue, where Bobby lives at 2161, is a short street lined on both sides with six-story apartment buildings. The apartments are all done in an English style—crenulated at the top, like castles, or decorated with dark beams and chunks of field stone, to give them a Shakespearean cottage feel, in theory. Bobby's building has a big compass of multicolored linoleum tiles on the lobby floor, an elevator with a diamond-shaped window, an awning and a doorman, at least until the war, when all the doormen go into the service. They never come back.

He has friends—Jack Goldberg, Herman Shapiro, Lenny Levinson, Sid Seidenstein. They are all Jewish and all live on Barnes Avenue. There is little reason to leave the block and hardly ever a need to leave the neighborhood. Jack is nearly a teenager before he realizes that most of the people in the world aren't Jewish, that everybody doesn't call noodles *luchtshen*.

At the end of the street is Pelham Parkway, a wide strip of trees and lawn and benches. The summer after his senior year in high school, Bobby studies there for his commercial radio license. His friend Sandy sits with him and they go over the six hundred questions on the test. They drill, drill, drill, so much that fifty years later she will be able to fire off the string, *dit dah dah, dit dit dah dah dah, dah dit dit, dah dit dit, dah dah*. W2DDM—Bobby's call letters.

Sandy is five foot three and cute, with short hair, the pony cut the girls are wearing. But she isn't Bobby's girlfriend. Nobody is. With the determination of a young monk he avoids what he considers "entangling alliances." You nail a girl, she gets in trouble, you have to marry her, and boom—you are in your father's sign shop for the rest of your life. Sandy ends up marrying Jack. But that comes later.

Rather than dating, they hang out in a big group. The Boys and the Girls is how Sandy thinks of it. They run into each other in the street and go sit in the park, or go sit in somebody's apartment. They talk about anything, everything. They're comfortable. If somebody has a question about sex—what's 69?—somebody else can probably answer it, based on something someone told them once.

Bobby loves classical music, and they troop to his apartment and sit on the floor on cushions with the lights out, listening to Ravel's *Bolero*, on four 45-rpm records, played on a portable player, its gray felt platter with a permanent spindle thick as a juice glass.

College looms. Morty didn't go, of course; he's getting a degree in

Advanced Sign Shop, with a minor in Jewelry Business. Sam assumes Bobby will do the same, once he settles down and stops acting crazy. A death sentence. Bobby thrashes harder as the net closes around him. The Fisher Body Division of General Motors has a yearly design competition: The Car of the Future. You design a car—Bobby's has infrared headlights and run-flat tires—then make a clay model, then use that to create a mold to make a plaster cast. It isn't exactly collecting three cereal boxtops, but Bobby gives it a shot. He labors over that plaster model—two feet long, black and white, streamlined as an egg, with voluptuous teardrop fenders. His father doesn't have an airbrush, so he brings it to one of his father's friends, who does. Eight coats of paint, sanding in between. His father tells him to send it in already. But it still isn't quite perfect to Bobby. The friend's airbrush isn't available, so Bobby uses his dad's Flitt gun to add a final coat of paint, and it goes on unevenly. Bobby tries to fix it in the sanding, but it doesn't come out quite right. A botch job. Time gone, Bobby boxes up the car and sends it to General Motors. He doesn't win.

Sam concedes that Bobby can go to college. Nothing fancy: Queens College, a commuter school, will do fine. Bobby starts out strong, then his grades crumble. The dean of students telephones his home. What's going on? Sam is embarrassed by the call. He says he has no idea.

What's going on is the apartment is loud. Doors are always slamming, the radio blasting. Bobby's still sharing a bedroom with Morty, who is almost twenty-two. Bobby tries to get the radio turned down and there are fights—arguments, sometimes fistfights between himself and Morty. During one epic battle they tire of hitting each other and go after each other's airplanes, hanging from the ceiling. In a moment, five hundred hours of work are gone, the ceiling air force reduced to broken, twisted heaps of matchsticks and stiff paper spread across the floor, both men crying, balling up each other's airplanes in their hands.

The dean's telephone call only makes things worse. Sam accuses

Bobby of embezzling the money given to him for books. What books? Where are the books? Show me. How much did each one cost?

Certain late afternoons, instead of studying, Bobby walks over to Van Cortlandt Park to watch the younger teenagers fly their model airplanes. Even from a distance he can identify each motion. The fuss over mixing the fuel, over setting the engine. A quick twist of the propeller. Then the spark, burp, and that continuous, soothing whine, like gas-powered mosquitoes as they take to the air, to swoop and strain at the ends of their tethers.

Bobby applies to Ohio State University, based on the fact that it is far away, relatively cheap, and his friend Lenny Levinson has started there and gives it a good report. His father vows he'll never pay for a fancy out-of-state school. "Not a nickel!" Sam shouts, finger twirling in the air like a Danny Kaye grandee. "Not a penny!"

But his mother says to Bobby, *sotto voce*, "*Go*. He'll pay. Don't worry. Just go and the money will be there."

Bobby also knows a guy there who is a member of the TEP fraternity—Jews—and of course Bobby will pledge TEP. Late in August, two future TEP brothers show up on Barnes Avenue in a big dark green, two-door Lincoln Continental to take him to school. They park the car right in front of 2161.

The whole street pauses to glance over and see who is getting in. Bobby takes his time loading his bag into the trunk. Too bad his father is at work, but word will get back. "They picked up Bobby in a Lincoln automobile!" He is in the big leagues now. Nevertheless, motoring west, he feels an odd twist: paired exhilaration and foreboding. Except for the previous summer, when he worked as a waiter in a girls' camp, and the four days he ran away and stayed at his cousin Freddy's house, he has never before been away from his family for more than a night or two. He is nineteen years old.

* * *

Freshman year passes at Ohio State. Bobby dates a girl named Jan Anderson, from McKeesport, Mississippi—a tough cookie who keeps a knife strapped to her ankle. Between her Southern drawl and the romance of that knife, you have to love her. No girls like that back on Barnes Avenue. To top it off, she gives Bobby the brushoff: "Come back when you grow up," she says.

From school, he writes to the Radio Operator's Union. He is a licensed commercial radio operator now, but not a union member since he has never been on a ship. Perhaps he can fill in for radio operators who want Christmas off? No, thank-you.

He quits the frat; they use the pledges as food servers, and between that and all the social events, Bobby doesn't have time to study, which he needs to do, badly. He wanted to get away from Barnes Avenue, and now he has, into the academic blender of Ohio State.

In the spring, he grows desperate. His father announces: if he doesn't want to work at the sign company, fine, don't work at the sign company. Sam has arranged for Bobby to get a summer job at a box factory. See if you like that better.

After reading his biography excerpted in a *Reader's Digest* found in the music room of the student union, Bobby writes to David Sarnoff, the head of the Radio Corporation of America and himself a former radio operator. He's trying to find a radio job on a ship, Bobby writes. Everyone else tells him that he needs to refer to a higher authority, so he thought he'd start at the top, with someone who doesn't have to look higher up for answers.

Sarnoff forwards the letter to RCA's Radiomarine Division, and a certain A. J. Costigan writes back. The letter arrives during finals, in a blue tissue airmail envelope. Costigan isn't encouraging. Hundreds of U.S. flag ships have been taken out of service. Radio jobs are tight. But he offers a single suggestion: try the training ship *Empire State*. Write to John Arkinstall at the New York Maritime College and give him your qualifications.

Bobby receives the letter May 23, 1952, in Columbus, a few days before the end of school. No time to write to Mr. Arkinstall. He'll have to phone.

Over the telephone, Mr. Arkinstall is friendly, enthusiastic, surprisingly so. Bob outlines his qualifications as a radio operator: he built his own 40-watt transmitter. He holds a commercial license. He says he can take thirty words a minute in Morse code, though the truth is closer to twenty-five. "Any commercial experience?" Mr. Arkinstall asks. None. "Ever been to sea?" No.

A silence on the line. Mr. Arkinstall asks when school is over. May 29. Can he be back in the Bronx, at the Maritime College, on June 2, 1 P.M., for an interview? Yes, he can. Fine, fine, come down to the ship, we'll talk more then.

Bobby hangs up the phone. He goes back to his room. The room seems different, portentous, like furniture set up on a stage at the beginning of a play.

CHAPTER 6

Freedom and the Sea

On May 30, Bobby takes a train from Columbus to the Bronx. The cornfields of Ohio give way to the scarred mountains of Pennsylvania and, at last, the factories and apartment buildings of the East. His parents are standing in the hubbub of Grand Central Terminal to meet him. He manages to wait until the car ride home to spring his big news.

"You're kidding, right?" Sam says, behind the wheel of his new Buick. "It's a wooden ship! It has sails. I did work out there. I wouldn't even step on it. I was afraid it would sink out from under me. It's a wooden ship. A ship made out of wood."

Bobby tries arguing with him, but the fact is, he doesn't know, not for certain. He has never seen the ship. He doesn't know. His father is a kibitzer, a teaser. But he doesn't seem to be teasing now. Bobby lets it go, uncertainty settling in his gut. A wooden ship?

By the time they get back to Barnes Avenue, they're fighting. Already. If I don't get on this ship, Bobby thinks, I'm never going to make it through the summer. He may not, anyway. A wooden ship or a box factory. Some choice. Just swell.

Fort Schuyler is only seven miles from Barnes Avenue. It would take fifteen minutes in a car. Bob doesn't dream of asking his dad. Instead he gives himself two hours to get there, changing buses twice. As the third bus nears Fort Schuyler, Bob is pressed against the window, looking. He sees a ship in the distance. Immediately, he sees one smokestack, which parallaxes into two. Metal. No sails. Not a wooden ship. Relief mixed with *you bastard.*

The *Empire State* is about one-tenth of a mile long, with a big superstructure of decks rising up from the midsection, looking almost too large for a ship of its size. A crane of some sort. Bobby walks up the gangway, finds someone to point him toward the radio room.

Mr. Arkinstall is writing in a log, a fan puttering away in the corner. He is a tall, thin man with friendly eyes, a high forehead, and wavy graying hair. In person, Mr. Arkinstall sizes up the slim, medium-built young man before him, an inch, maybe two, under six feet tall. Mr. Arkinstall asks Bob if he is willing to take the morning and evening watches. Of course, Bob says. Can he check the emergency batteries every day, and help maintain the radar? Of course—he is a physics major; just finished his freshman year. The pay is $90 a week. Will that do? Bob says the pay seems fine.

They shake hands. Mr. Arkinstall sends him to the college doctor, immediately, to get his physical, which consists of stripping naked, touching his toes, then getting dressed. "You pass, welcome aboard," the doctor says. Mr. Arkinstall tells Bob to go to Harry Sadow Naval Uniform Specialists, on Church Street across from the Naval District Headquarters in lower Manhattan—nowhere else—and buy three uniforms: two khaki, one white, and a pair of black military dress shoes. "Tell him you're on the *Empire State* and they'll take care of you," Mr. Arkinstall says. They sail next Wednesday—a week from tomorrow—

with the tide. Plan to be here Friday, in khaki uniform, for orientation, and every day after that.

Bob is back on the pier, repeating the name of the uniform store to himself, when he realizes that he has no idea where the ship is going.

His father made a promise. "If my son gets that job, I'll eat my hat," Sam Steinberg said the morning Bobby went to meet Mr. Arkinstall aboard the *Empire State*. Now that Bobby has the job, however, he knows better than to try to call in his father's wager. He'd like to—to feed him the hat, forcibly, starting with the brim and working his way to the crown, saving the feather for last. But he doesn't.

Anyway, Bobby is used to his father reneging on promises. A decade earlier, when he was a boy, Sam had promised him a real Lionel train set if he spent his Saturdays working at the sign shop. Sam was so bold as to say that he had the train set, already, waiting on a high shelf. Bobby, not yet ten, did the work, woke up at 5 A.M. on Saturday mornings to mix paints and clean brushes—for a year. But he never got the train set. Turned out, there was no train set. There had never been one.

Forever after, he would be haunted by that phantom train set, as if he could see it, up in the dark heights of his parents' bedroom closet, waiting, a big Lionel box with a painting of some lucky, loved boy on the lid, playing delightedly with his trains in front of the glowing hearth.

The job of second radio operator on the *Empire State* is not in Sam Steinberg's control, however. He cannot withhold it and is too smart to try. What he does is immediately identify the flaw, the weakness. Granted, the ship is not made of wood, as he had supposed—he was thinking of the *St. Mary*, Maritime's ship in the 1920s. But still, the fact that the job is open a week before the ship sails means it has to be lousy. No question about it. Means that nobody else wants the job, nobody else asked for it. Sam happily expounds on the lousiness of this job, the unreliability of the ship, the certainty of doom. If the State of New York owns it, the ship has got to be a rusty tin can. It'll probably sink—straight to the bottom. Bobby will come swimming home, if he comes back at all.

Sam keeps this up, gleeful, at every opportunity, right to the moment Bobby needs to go downtown to buy his uniforms. Then he grumbles and produces a wad of money and loans his son cash to buy the clothing. Give Sam Steinberg credit for that. As bottomlessly cheap, as famously cheap as he without question is, when the crucial moment comes, he coughs up the dough. A loan, certainly. To be paid back, in full, from the first paycheck. Absolutely. But he parts with the cash, and that, to Bobby, is a redemptive miracle of kindness.

Bobby does not go to Harry Sadow Naval Uniform Specialists. He goes to Berkowitz's Government Surplus on Houston Street, taking the subway down with his friend, Sid. The clerk—a short, fat, balding Jew wearing a fat necktie with a fat mermaid on it—hustles over, rubbing his hands.

Uniforms? We've got uniforms. It's a uniform store. Police. Army. Navy. Whatever you want. Bobby says he needs three naval uniforms, two khaki and one dress white.

"So we start with the khaki," says the man, reaching up with a long pole to hook a uniform on a hanger about ten feet off the ground.

"How much?" Bobby says. "Forty-five dollars," the bald man says. Sid sticks his finger in his ear and twists, looking at Bobby, crossing his eyes, and sticking the tip of his tongue out of the corner of his mouth. Bobby doesn't need the hint.

"If I wanted comedy, I'd listen to the radio," he says, trying to give bass and authority to the phrase he has heard his father say dozens of times. "I'll give you nine dollars."

The clerk's eyes widen with genuine feigned surprise. "Nine dollars?

Why don't you just stick me up and take it? Nine dollars. Help-police-I'm-being-robbed. Thirty-eight dollars."

And so it goes, back and forth, a kind of ballet. Bob gets the khakis, the whites—*new* whites—the shoes, the hat. He walks out with everything for $115. Harry Sadow Naval Uniform Specialists? *Das ken nor a goyim.*

Bobby enters the apartment quietly and walks back to his bedroom—windows open, warm late spring breeze ruffling the curtains. He sets the parcel down, opens it, unfolds the white uniform. He's almost afraid to touch it. So dazzling white. He pulls on the pants. He gives the shoes a last buff and slips them on. He slides into the jacket and buttons it, first admiring the shoulder boards, with their single stripe and the seal of the New York State Maritime College, embroidered in gold. He lifts the hat from its box, between his flat palms, like a 78 record, and sets it carefully on his head, then grabs the brim and the back and adjusts it, minusculely.

Bobby can't see himself fully in the little mirror over his dresser, so he steps out into the hall, heading toward the bathroom. His mother, dusting in the living room, notices him.

"Bobby!" she says, with a bit of a gasp. He steps into the living room, beaming. Bobby stands straight, plucking the cap off his head. He holds it awkwardly for a moment, then tucks it under his arm, as if he had done it before. He turns to model. His mother stands there, tears in her eyes, suppressing her smile, clamping down on it, as if she wants to but knows she shouldn't. Shaking her head in wonder, fingertips pressed against her cheeks, looking at her son, who looks back at her, both of them saying nothing.

June 10, 1952, is an exciting day to be on a ship. The brand-new S.S. *United States* is, at that very moment, steaming hell-bent for Portsmouth, setting a record for a ship crossing the Atlantic that will never be broken. Three days plus change. And that isn't even at top speed. The top speed is classified, a military secret. The crossing is big front-page news.

Bob sprints up the gangway of the *Empire State*, top speed a pokey 20 knots, ready for his last day of training before the ship sails—to Bermuda, as it turns out, then Spain, then Greece, then France, then back to Spain again, then home. He turns, and almost smacks into a pair of cadets, stripped to the waist, on their knees, scrubbing the deck with big brushes. They all gape at each other. After a moment of shock, Bob places the cadets: Harry Kessler and Bill Weiss, two jerks from his homeroom at Christopher Columbus High School.

They haven't seen each other for a year. Weiss and Kessler have been attending the Maritime Academy, intensively preparing for their careers as merchant sailors. This will be their shakedown cruise, and they will be doing it as seamen, first class—the grunt workmen of the waves. Bobby Steinberg, having spent a year studying physics at Ohio State in landlocked Columbus, Ohio, will be an ensign, ranking only a little above them, but above them all the same. Their boss.

"What the fuck are you doing here, Steinberg?" one of them says, unpleasantly, setting down his brush and standing up, radiating menace.

That, Bobby thinks, is a good question.

At breakfast that last morning, Sam grandly announces that he is taking the morning off work to drive Bobby to the pier. Frances smiles knowingly. Bobby is astonished. This is as big a gesture as his father is capable of, and his springing it at the last minute is his way of heightening the drama. A surprise.

Bobby inventories his sea bag one last time. He looks around his room: the ceiling, oddly empty, the receiver, which now seems so small. A child's toy, on the desk he made himself.

It's time. Bobby and his parents walk the half block to the garage and call for the Buick, which swoops down the ramp. They stash the big sea bag in the trunk. His brother, plus Sid and Jack, crowd in the back with him, and they drive down the Hutchinson River Parkway, turn into East Tremont Avenue, and take it all the way to Fort Schuyler. The pier, which had been so sparse and functional when Bobby was going to his orientation the preceding week, is now crowded with cadets, most with a little knot of kin.

Bobby stows his bag aboard ship, checks in with Mr. Arkinstall, then goes to say good-bye to his family and friends.

Hugs and kisses and handshakes. What strikes Bobby most is how cool his mother seems. Not crying, not upset. Instead, she steps back to shoot the scene with a movie camera. Bobby has never seen her use it before—usually Morty does—and is surprised that she knows how. He walks up the gangway, then stands at the rail to wave. His mother calls out "smile," but Bobby, tight-faced, shakes his head back and forth. He can't smile.

In the moments before the *Empire State II* sails, Bob and the other officers and crew assemble on her deck. The president of the college, Vice Admiral Calvin T. Durgin, USN (Ret.) makes a short speech, urging the cadets to take advantage of this unique opportunity to learn the ways of the sea and to always remember their special role abroad.

"You are first and foremost Americans," he says. "You must seize every opportunity, in foreign ports, to demonstrate the deportment and friendliness expected of representatives of the United States of America, and to display a genuine interest in the affairs of your foreign hosts."

Bob finds Durgin's words oddly stirring, although he notices that one of the engineers, a broad-chested, bowlegged guy, Jerry somebody, closes his eyes, drops his chin to his chest, and joggles his shoulders, as if he were laughing.

*　*　*

Ships pitch, which is the motion of tipping forward and back, forward and back, as they cut into the waves. If the waves are big enough, a person standing on the deck of a ship, staring straight ahead, sees first the sky, then the bottom of a watery trough, then the sky, then the trough.

Ships also roll. Rolling is the side-to-side motion. So if you are looking straight ahead, the horizon is not steady and flat, but tilts back and forth.

And finally, ships yaw, which is the combined effect of pitching and rolling, used to describe various plunges and sudden off-axis twists of a ship that are neither forward and backward nor side to side, but somewhere in between.

In addition to pitching, rolling, and yawing, the *Empire State* is a snapper. She had been the *Hydrus* during the war, an assault cargo ship that carried landing craft. When she became the *Empire State II* and was refitted, they permanently loaded tons of pig-iron ballast in her hold, trying to make her more stable by compensating for the cargo that was no longer there—well, mostly not there. She is carrying some cargo, such as one thousand pounds of hard candy, a gift to needy European youngsters purchased by the college's Protestant Club.

The result of the pig iron—and, to a lesser extent, the candy—is that a strong wave tips the *Empire State* in one direction, where she pauses a moment, as if making up her mind, before gravity grabs the tons of pig iron in her round-bottomed, shallow-draft keel and yanks the ship back with a snap. It is not a pleasant sensation.

The largest water-born vessel Bob has been on prior to putting out to sea on the *Empire State* was a rowboat on the small lake in Van Cortlandt Park. Rowboats on park lakes do not pitch, roll, yaw, or snap.

On top of everything, the first night out, after stopping at Fort Pond Bay to set the gyroscope, a storm blows up: a nor'easter. Green seas break over the bow. The ship rolls a full 30 degrees—so violently that the magnetic compass and binnacle tear loose from their pedestal and crash across the bridge. Luckily nobody is killed. The mugs—fresh cadets—add a new dimension to the word *green*. So many are seasick so violently that Captain Olivet orders them not to hang over the rail, puking, out of fear that one of them will be lost over the side as the ship rolls. One mess call nobody shows up.

The radio shack is at the tallest part of the ship, and the rolling is most pronounced there. Bob has to man his station, ready to signal in an emergency, which he expects at any moment.

Captain Olivet diverts south, reduces speed, then heaves to—something he hates to do because it wastes time—and rides out the storm for more than five hours. Finally the weather breaks, and he can make a run for it.

One guy is so seasick he has to be taken off the ship via running boat as soon as the storm subsides and hauled back into port for the long, humiliating trek home. At least, thinks Bob, clutching at the desk in the radio room, that isn't me. That isn't me that isn't me that isn't me that isn't me.

After the *Empire State* leaves Fort Pond Bay, steaming southward, Bob lurches through the foul metal passageways, bouncing off bulkheads, stumbling over the high lip of doorways, trying to get his sea legs while attempting to figure out if the person coming toward him is sick and should be avoided or an officer and should be saluted. He is worried more about being seen falling than about falling, and he does both. The ship seems to time its strongest lunges for moments when somebody is looking at him or talking to him. He has to shoot an arm out to steady himself while the officer in front of him, accustomed to the sea, stares quizzically, as if Bob were having some sort of seizure.

At the end of that first awful day, when he takes his shirt off in his quarters, Bob sees in the mirror that his shoulders and elbows are black and blue. This is the end of the same day that he referred to the belowdecks section of the ship as "the basement." One day down. Three months to go.

The sailors on the *Empire State* call Bob "Sparky," the generic tag for radio operators since Old West days, when a telegraph actually tossed off a spark of electricity with every dot or dash. It is an affectionate term, but there is something juvenile about it as well. Mr. Arkinstall, for instance, a lieutenant commander in the Naval Reserve who sailed the deadly North Atlantic run during World War II, is not a "Sparky."

Bob grows to enjoy the nickname, to enjoy the routines of shipboard life—once the weather clears—during the three-day trip to Bermuda. He learns to plant his feet, wide, while sitting at one of the two long, green felt-covered tables in the officers' mess (the felt helps keep the plates from sliding). He learns to take his bite when the ship is at full roll, in that pause before it rocks back in the other direction. Less reconstituted egg on your face that way.

He checks the specific gravity of the radio batteries—one of his duties. The batteries are outside, just aft of the radio shack, in a boxlike compartment. He learns to check the batteries without splashing the acid on himself. He learns to stand upwind, but not before his uniforms are peppered with pinholes. Bob also learns the difference between 9 volts, the battery current he used to run his key in his bedroom in the Bronx, and 115 volts, the generator voltage the ship's key is plugged into. A telegraph key is closing a simple circuit. The first time Bob wires his Vibroplex key into the ship's system, his finger strays off the red Bakelite pad and touches the bare contact—not long enough to kill him, fortunately, but long enough to send him leaping out of the chair, hopping around, and shaking his singed finger. It is a learning experience. He covers the contact with electrical tape.

Other than death by electrocution, Bob's biggest fear is that he'll screw up the Morse code transcriptions so badly that he'll be put off the ship after it docks in Bermuda and sent home. After the big farewell, he'll be back on Barnes Avenue in a week, jobless and humiliated. His father would love that.

There is a relentlessness to Morse code. It keeps coming. A moment's confusion, a bit of hesitation or distraction, and you're lost. Sure, you can ask the sender to repeat something, once or twice. But do that too much and you brand yourself an amateur.

Bobby is genuinely worried, dreading the moment Mr. Arkinstall sets him before the radio console and lets him handle the messages coming and going. The hourly weather reports come in at thirty words per minute—faster than he can comfortably transcribe, though most of the transmission is numbers, which are easier.

But it never happens. Mr. Arkinstall tells him to get accustomed to the routines of shipboard life; he will handle the radio traffic until the ship leaves Bermuda. Then Bob can begin his regular 8 A.M. to 12 P.M. and 8 P.M. to 12 A.M. shifts. A great relief to Bob. That means they can't fire him at least until the ship gets to Europe.

The technical aspects of the ship—the radio room and the corridors—are only the beginning, however. There are also the social shoals of being on a ship. Bob quickly realizes that, before he opens his mouth, he has three strikes against him. Strike one, he is young—at nineteen, the youngest officer by nearly a decade, younger than two-thirds of the cadets. Like the mugs, he has never been to sea. But he is not a cadet; he is not attending New York Maritime.

That is strike two: he is a summer sailor, taking the place of a career seaman who otherwise would have—at least in many people's minds—gotten the job. More than one shipmate feels compelled to tell Bob this. His job should have gone to a legitimate sailor, and would have had Bob not somehow clouted it for himself.

The rumor is that he is related to RCA head David Sarnoff—

perhaps his nephew or even his son, under an assumed name. Bob does not actively try to dispel this rumor, figuring it will work in his favor, not realizing it paints him, not entirely unfairly, as a pampered, inexperienced rich Jew on a summer lark.

That is strike three: he is Jewish. The only Jewish officer at a time when genteel—and not so genteel—antisemitism is still the norm, despite the sobering slap of the war. It is a feeling that can be contained, usually, but tends to come out when they're drinking. And officers on the ship drink constantly. There is nothing clandestine about it. Olivet has a wet bar in his quarters. Other officers sit in their cabins on their off-duty hours with big pitchers of gin and ice on the small desks, playing solitaire and sipping. What else is there to do?

Bob certainly doesn't get off to a rousing start with his roommate. Bob is sitting at one of the tiny, fold-out desks, arranging his stuff when the curtained door to the cabin slides aside and a little white-haired man steps in. Bob stands up and begins to introduce himself.

"I know who you are," says the man, casting a critical look around the room. "Arkinstall told me all about you. I'm George Riser. We'll get along, if you follow the rules. The top bunk is mine. The desk you're sitting at is mine. My locker is to the left. This room will be kept neat as a pin, and we won't have any trouble."

With that he leaves. Bob slowly sinks down on the chair, then springs back up again, looking down at it as if he had sat on a tack, and begins moving his stuff to the other desk.

Bermuda strikes Bob as a fairyland. The pink coral houses. The giant palms. He digs into his limited vocabulary of metaphor and comes up with "The Wizard of Oz."

In port, the radio room is shut down. Bob's job becomes hanging out at beach clubs, swimming in the ocean, picking up local girls and dancing with them in the evening. The men on the *Empire State*, like sailors everywhere, pride themselves on their ability to descend upon ports, locustlike, and strip them of their women. The year before, in France, a cadet distinguished himself by trying to pick up a woman on her honeymoon. He nearly succeeded.

All the girls want to see the ship. Bob loves it when the officer on deck salutes him, smartly, as he steps off the running boat with his date. Boy, oh boy, talk about making an impression.

He pauses from the whirl to grab an elegant sheet of Belmont Manor Hotel and Golf Club stationery and craft this carefully modulated knife to slip into Morty, back in the Bronx:

Dear Brother,

Just thought I'd drop you a line. Tonight I went ashore with one of the officers. We went to the Elbow Beach Club. From there I came to the Belmont Manor. Bermuda is truly a wonderful spot for a honeymoon and maybe someday I'll get a chance to come back in that capacity. By the way, I want to thank you for coming down with Mom to see me off. I hope the movies you took come out. I noticed there was a write-up in the papers about our departure, did you perchance see it? So far I have led a somewhat interesting week. I am treated with courtesy and respect due my rank, it is simply amazing.

As far as my job goes, it is both interesting and since it is new to me I find it somewhat difficult. I imagine all new things are difficult to begin with, however, as one progresses it becomes much easier. Unlike all the other officers, I have four days off with pay. All told, I get about a month off with pay which is pretty good, don't you agree?

I am told, since I am traveling on a government vessel, when we hit the various foreign ports there will be various official functions that the officers will attend such as cocktail parties etc. Before we en-

ter a port we notify the American embassy at that port of call. He arranges the rest. After we leave Bermuda we will be at sea two weeks before we reach Baeleric Islands. If you get a chance, drop me a line.

Robert

"Robert." Up to that point he was always "Bobby."

Robert does have one job in Bermuda. He is delegated to go ashore and collect the duty-free Canadian Club. At an officers' meeting, his name is put forward as shore mess secretary, and all hands shoot up. Obviously, the fix is in, though Bob isn't sure why and can't bring himself to ask. His suspicion is that he, alone among the officers, did not sign up for any whiskey, therefore he can be trusted with its distribution. Sailor's logic.

Bob isn't a teetotaler. He sips gin fizzes in Bermuda, on dates, since he is thirsty from dancing and doesn't trust the water. But never enough to get drunk. Bob has been drunk exactly twice in his life, up to that point, and remembers each incident vividly.

The first time he is nine years old. At the reception following his brother's bar mitzvah. He and his cousin Freddy are bored, running around the tables at Senate Caterers, 188th Street and the Grand Concourse, ignored in the commotion. They come upon a table holding a tray of shot glasses filled with Crown Royal. Freddy dares him. Bob downs one shot, then another.

His mother calls to him. "It's starting now Bobby, come on." She leads him by the hand to the platform at the front of the synagogue.

The rabbi is chanting. The congregation is standing. Bobby goes to stand and suddenly feels light-headed. "I think I'm going to faint, Ma," he says. The world spins, condenses to a point, fades to black.

He's laid out in the ladies' room. His mother calls for smelling salts—a big commodity in those days—but none of the ladies have any.

His mother's sister, the hefty Tante Brana, slips into a stall and pees on a handkerchief, and they clamp it over Bobby's face. That brings him to, eyes popping, pushing the handkerchief away from his nose.

Not a lot of drinking after that. Years pass before he and Jack, Herman, and Sid are at his apartment, by themselves, on a summer afternoon. They decide to take a bottle of his parents' Manischewitz, add ice cubes and pineapple—as if it weren't sweet enough already—and then drink the stuff. The results are the same, except no Tante Brana to bring him around.

Bob collects the money, goes ashore, buys the ten cases of Canadian Club, has them delivered to the ship, signs for them, wheels them around the officers' quarters, and distributes the square brown bottles to his grateful fellow officers.

He does have a drink. Along with the Canadian Club, he buys a case of Dry Sack sherry for himself. After his shift is over, he pours himself exactly four ounces and drinks it, at the noontime and at the midnight shift change, sitting outside the radio room, relieved to be done for the time being.

That's okay, first because "sack" is mentioned in Shakespeare so it isn't the same as whiskey. Jews don't drink whiskey—not unless they're celebrating something. And second, the sack is medicinal, a tonic. His stomach is killing him.

Mr. Arkinstall is true to his word. Once they leave Bermuda, Bob begins taking the traffic, monitoring the shore station—WCC Chatham Radio—listening for his ship's call letters, pairing off with an operator on a different frequency when there are messages to relay. The Chatham operators are good; they quickly sense Bob's level of ability and slow to it. But the official Navy weather report—the one used to generate the big weather charts used to navigate the ship—still comes in at exactly thirty words a minute, a word consisting of five numbers in this case, sent over in blocks of 100 five-digit numbers. If Bob misses a number, the whole weather map the numbers are generating can be misplotted. Captain Olivet could sail into a typhoon he thinks he is skirting. Bob suspects—all right, knows, in his gut, literally—that he isn't the kind of radio operator he wants to be. Not that guy from the Ellsberg books—the cool, efficient Sparky he once imagined he would be, calmly tapping out the distress signal as all hell breaks loose around him. Not a seasoned pro like Mr. Arkinstall, who can key a story from the *New York Times* as fast as you can read it aloud. Bobby fears that he is incompetent and soon people will find out. The Dry Sack helps.

Captain Olivet is not a man you want to send into a hurricane. He is a hurricane all by himself: a tight man who runs a tight ship. You do not saunter onto his bridge. You wouldn't want to even if he permitted it, which he does not. Bob thinks of him as a headwaiter in khakis. Short, prim, with a thin mustache, he'll chew you out three different ways for a scuff on your shoe. Just try wearing white socks with your uniform; he'll go berserk. Olivet acts as dean of students at Fort Schuyler during the school year, and is famous for giving chase to a group of cadets he caught breaking into a building. The cadets bolted across campus, with Olivet hot after them, waving his little arms, shrieking. "Stop! This is your captain speaking! Stop! Stop! I command you!"

Bob dreads his encounters with Olivet, which as a radio operator are frequent.

After his second shift, at midnight, Bob sometimes flips on the auto-alarm, takes his chair outside of the radio shack, set high between the smokestacks, and watches the ship cut through the sea, the white wake rolling out against dark Atlantic waters.

He can't look straight ahead or behind—the stacks are in the way—so he tends to stare off at the horizon, marked only by a vague meeting of the deep black ocean with the softer coal velvet of the sky with its flickering sequin field of stars.

Taking nips of Dry Sack against the midnight chill, Bob scans the vast expanse and gently marvels at the fate that blew him here from the Bronx.

Bob is tired, staring out at nothing at all, thinking nothing at all, when he sees it: an orange flare, far away, streaking straight up and exploding. A distress rocket. He stands up, startled, almost kicking over his Dry Sack. The rocket is already fading. He hurries to the bridge, flying through the corridors. Captain Olivet is not there; the mate on watch didn't see anything and doesn't care. Bob walks over to the door of Olivet's quarters, behind the bridge. Hesitating a moment, fist pulled back and cocked, at shoulder level, he raps on the door. After a long wait, he knocks again. Captain Olivet opens the door, grumbling, then grumbles more when he hears what's the matter. Wrestling on a robe, he walks out to the bridge. Bob follows, gropingly, the bridge lit by only a few red lights to preserve night vision. The captain stares out at the black windows, then down at the sweeping bright green line of the radar scope, then at Ensign Steinberg. "There's nothing there," he says, his face reflecting green from the scope.

Agitated, Bob begins to explain that, of course, a small boat wouldn't show up on the radar. But the captain cuts him off. "I don't *see* anything." He gives Bob a hard look, then turns and strides back into his cabin. The door slams. Bob turns to the mate on watch, as if in appeal. The mate turns wordlessly away.

Bob spends his days busily copying messages from WCC Chatham. Instructions from the school. News of babies born and scores from ballgames. And tragedy. The father of a cadet has died suddenly. Bob types the cadet's name on the envelope. He rereads the terse, staccato message. "REGRET TO INFORM YOU FATHER PASSED AWAY TUESDAY. . . ." The message seems so stark against the fire-engine-red letterhead, a bold RCA ending in a zigzagging *A*. ("Radiogram

Radio Marine Corporation of America, a Service of Radio Corporation of America: Ship to Ship; Ship to Shore; Shore to Ship; Fast;
Accurate.")

Bob folds the sheet of paper and inserts it in the envelope. It is his
job to deliver messages to their recipients. Bob usually does this at the
end of his shift, grabbing a handful of sealed envelopes and making his
rounds through the ship. But a death seems like something that can't
wait and, switching on the auto-alarm, Bob heads aft. Down a few
staircases, into the depths of the ship, where the cadets sleep, four deep
on canvas bunks. After a few tries, he gets close enough to the proper
area that one of the guy's buddies points out the bed. The cadet isn't
there. Bob wonders if he should deliver it personally, then sets the envelope, carefully, on the thin pillow resting on the neatly made gray
wool blanket. Bob gives the envelope a last look: a time bomb. Then
he heads back up to the radio room.

Later that day, still shaken from the experience, Bob sits down to
write his father, telling him about the message:

> *Dad, I know that talking to you is like talking to a stone wall. . . . It
> served to remind me of your stubborn refusal to see the doctor. All I
> can say to myself is will you have to learn the hard way? It seems a
> characteristic trait of the Steinbergs is a pig-headed stubbornness.
> Can't you see it in your brothers? Can't you once listen to reason?
> God, if you cannot listen to reason then I just do not know what to
> say. For once be a little different than most of the Steinbergs and use
> a little common sense and see the doctor for a checkup. I don't mean
> to offend you but what else can I say?*

The *Empire State II* reaches the Strait of Gibraltar on June 28, and
slows to toss a wreath into the water in honor of Captain Jones
Hodgeson Budd, a bigwig in the maritime post of the American Le-
gion. Bob, who has never seen any continent other than his own,

is now seeing two more—Europe to port and Africa to starboard, though he still gets those terms confused. The gap between the continents is just seven miles wide.

They also toss something else. One of Bob's duties is to haul the suitcase-sized emergency transmitter to his lifeboat during drills. The drills are every two weeks. The crew assembles on the heaving deck, in their life jackets, from the senior officers down to the ship's dog, Skippy. Someone has made a little orange life vest for Skippy, and his owner, the executive officer Commander James Maley, religiously puts the vest on the dog for drills.

The suitcase radio is supposed to float. That's what it says on the side: EMERGENCY RADIO—FLOATABLE. But it strikes Bob, dragging the thing to the boats, that it's awfully heavy to float. Mr. Arkinstall, who has lifted it himself, has to agree. He was in the Navy long enough to know that to ask a question like that is to answer it, but he still arranges for a test.

After the wreath ceremony, before the ship picks up steam again, they lower the port running boat ramp and clatter down the stairs to the water level—Bob, lugging the heavy transmitter, a cadet holding a boathook, and Mr. Arkinstall.

With a nod from Mr. Arkinstall, Bob uses both hands and flings the radio into the water. It makes a splash and sinks instantly. The cadet with the hook sweeps it over the water but the radio is gone, trailing bubbles. "Well, now we know," says Mr. Arkinstall, and they troop back up the stairs. The next day they are due in Palma de Majorca, Spain.

CHAPTER 7

The Salty Kiss

The sun is brighter in Spain. The day after passing through the Strait of Gibraltar, the *Empire State II* arrives in Palma de Majorca, one of the Balearic Islands. Looking ashore through a porthole is like staring into the eye of a furnace.

If Bermuda struck Bob as a Wonderland version of the Flagler—the Catskills resort his family summered at after they outgrew the Lake House—then Spain is off the scale, another planet—Mars or, better yet, Venus. Narrow streets. Windows with wooden shutters, bright colors faded to charming pastel, closed tight against the blinding midday sun. Steam-driven taxi cabs. High, square horse-drawn carts. Women wrapped in black silk shawls.

The officers tumble off the ship in their dress whites, paper collars soaking through almost immediately in the heat. They head to the bars, they head to the brothels. The beaches are rocky, so Bob heads to the pool at the nautical club—El Club Nautico. Every Spanish port has one, run by the port authority. There he can strip off the uniform in a small room, leave it on a hanger, guarded by an old woman for a few *pesetas*, and sit by the poolside in his bathing suit, taking a sunbath.

Bob studied Spanish for a year in high school and a year in college, which puts him at an advantage when picking up girls. His shipmates trust him to translate for them, which is a mistake. Bob delights in inserting a delicate layer of clumsiness into their pickup lines. "He says you are beautiful," Bob earnestly intones, his shipmate nodding eagerly beside him. "Almost as beautiful as his mother . . ."

The U.S. Embassy acts as a social director for the ship, rounding up nice girls for dances; the girls dance with the officers and the seniors, the underclassmen get the chaperons and the mothers. Bob meets a young lady at a dance: Conchita Guiterez del Almo. Her father is commandant of the Spanish Merchant Marine. She has red hair, swept up, and speaks no English. At first sight Bob thinks of Carmen, from the opera. They arrange to go out dancing the next night. Bob shows up, 7:30 P.M., at her house—ten rooms with an elevator. Bob is ushered into the dim, tiled living room and the family files in. First the father, then the mother, then the cousins, then Conchita, wearing a white lace dress with a train that trails several feet behind her. Bob's first thought, accompanied by a flash of panic, is: *a wedding dress.* But that can't be. Following her is an elderly woman draped in black, walking three feet behind—her *duenna*. It seems like something out of a movie.

For a moment Bob thinks they are all going to come along, en masse. But it is just he and Conchita, and of course the *duenna*, in the back of her father's cavernous black limousine. Bob can't believe it. Conchita is wearing an ermine wrap.

They dance. They smile at each other. She has to be back home by 10. In the limousine on the way back, with the *duenna* napping, or discreetly pretending to, Bob attempts to take Conchita's hand. She draws her hand away. It is not the custom, Robert, she says. When, he asks, would it be the custom? If we are married, she says, then it will be the custom.

Still, they go out every night for the next three nights. Bob speaks enough Spanish for them to get into political arguments on the benefits of Franco fascism versus American democracy. Conchita gets agitated, answers very fast, and Bob struggles to keep up, eventually passing his little pocket dictionary to her to find the word he is having trouble with. Thus the evenings dissolve into a whirl of dancing, of smiling, of hotly passing the dictionary back and forth.

During the day, he wanders Majorca. He meets a man from the Arabian American Oil Company who asks him to dinner at the Hotel Majorca, where he sees a sketch by van Gogh. The sailors are advised not to drink the water in Palma, so Bob takes his hydration through gin fizzes, at 4 *pesetas*—about 10 cents—a glass. He buys his mother a shawl.

One afternoon he and another man he met—a banker's son enjoying a Spanish lark after college—rent a little boat to row around the harbor. They are drinking a bottle of *vino tinto* and singing Spanish songs. Bob has his shirt off and his pants rolled up and is wearing a big straw hat. They row toward the *Empire State*. As they approach the ship, the officer of the deck waves them off, shouting, "Away, Spaniards!" Bob loves that. From Bobby in the Bronx to Roberto the Spaniard in three weeks flat. Fantastic.

That delicious image doesn't last long back on the *Empire State*. His second night in Palma, Bob is waiting on the dock for the launch to take him back to the ship. It isn't late—just after 10 P.M. An officer from the ship's store, Lt. Harry Kessler, Sr.—the father of his classmate from high school—is there waiting.

"Good evening, lieutenant," Bob says, with an easy salute. The lieutenant stares at him, mouth hanging open.

"You dirty Jew bastard," he slurs. Bob looks at him. Stinko drunk. A wine stain the size of a baby bib around his neck. Kessler is standing, unsteadily, with his back to the water. Bob is stone sober. A quick step forward and a hard push, Bob thinks, is all it would take, and the lieutenant would be in the drink. He tenses up, as if to do it. But his mind, already racing, skips to the next few steps—the shout, the splash, the inquiry. A slur can be denied far easier than a shove into the harbor. Bob turns away, saying nothing.

After the running boat takes them to the ship, Kessler climbs the stairs, salutes the officer on duty, takes a single step forward, and pitches face down onto the deck. Out cold. A few cadets run over to hoist him belowdecks. "It was here," the yearbook later deadpans, of Majorca generally, "that the deck hands gained practical experience in hauling human cargo aboard."

The next morning, Bob wakes clear-headed but with a certain sense of dread sloshing around his stomach from his encounter with Kessler the night before. He can't have it hanging over his head. At breakfast, he makes a point of stepping in front of Lt. Kessler and making eye contact. "Hi, Bob," Kessler says, brightly, peeling an egg, not a trace of the glowering malice of the day before, the wine stain passably camouflaged with talcum powder. He doesn't remember. Bob lets it go.

The *Empire State* sails from Palma on July 7—too soon for Bob, too late for the engineering cadet who, the day before, accidentally cuts off his thumb on a band saw in the machine shop. The cadet stuns his crewmates by quietly picking up the thumb and carrying it himself to sick bay, walking unaided, his maimed hand tucked under his armpit, his other palm out, open, as if he were asking for alms and the severed thumb is what Fate had given him. A faraway sort of a smile on his face that will haunt everybody who sees it.

It is a five-day trip to Venice up the Adriatic, and before the *Empire State* has gone halfway much of the crew is sick with dysentery and diarrhea, picked up from the water in Spain. Bob's gin fizzes protect him. In fact, he has the opposite problem. As difficult as the food is to put in (his mother's cooking spoiled him), it has a very hard time getting out.

It doesn't help that, for all the concerns about rank and formality, the officers' restroom on the *Empire State II* consists of four toilets, two by two, facing each other, without benefit of a barrier or stall of any kind. You have to sit and look at each other. Small wonder he has the problem he has. And he has been losing weight the whole trip; his uniforms hang on him.

Bob doesn't ask what the doctor gives him, but it works like a stick of dynamite. He is himself again, eating dried prunes by the handful as the ship sails into the Grand Canal and docks one hundred yards off Piazza San Marco—Saint Mark's Square.

Venice has traffic as bad as Manhattan's, a jumble of motorized gondolas, pole boats, bumboats—boats of all description, jostling and racing around each other. There is a party at the embassy that night, and officials come aboard at twilight to escort the *Empire State*'s officers ashore. Captain Olivet, in a jovial mood—they say he has a mistress in Venice—asks Bob to come along in his private launch, with the tassels hanging from the trim. As they pull away from the *Empire State*, the semaphore lamp on another U.S. ship, a navy cruiser docked across the canal, starts up, blinking out a signal light from the bridge wing.

"Tell us what they're saying, Sparky," the captain says, clapping Bob on the knee. Bob has never read a semaphore in his life—the Morse code is the same, but blinks are different than clicks: eyes versus ears. Everyone in the running boat looks at him. Bobby picks up a pair of binoculars to buy time.

"Always . . ." he says, as if deciphering the code, "buy . . . Chesterfields." The captain roars. The others laugh. He's off the hook.

Commander Maley's dog, a two-year-old cocker spaniel named Skippy, bounds up the ship's ladders and negotiates the decks in a sideways waddle when the sea is rough. Captain Olivet, in a curious lapse, lets him sleep on the bridge because—Jerry Doyle says—Skippy's the only one on the ship even shorter than the captain.

As the most junior officer, and since the radio room is shut down in port and he has nothing else to do, it is Bob's duty to exercise Skippy. Living in the Bronx, Bob has never had a dog and doesn't think much of them. Dogs are dirty. It is humiliating to sit in the running boat, holding Skippy in his lap, one hand clasping the collar, worried about being crapped on or that, in a moment of exuberance, the stupid animal will plunge into the Grand Canal and drown.

And Skippy is an exuberant dog, yipping and yapping and straining at his leash after the boat deposits Bob and Skippy at the foot of St. Mark's Square. Skippy takes off, Bob yanked after him, one hand instinctively grabbing at his cap. Then Skippy stops, sniffs, and takes off again, between the twin columns of Egyptian granite that mark the formal entrance to the city, the columns of Marco and Todaro. Finally, Skippy finds fascination at the column to the left, the one holding the three-ton winged lion, the proud symbol of Venice. Byron wrote of "The winged lion's marble piles, where Venice sat in state, throned on her hundred isles!"

Skippy studies the base of the column, sniffs it, then raises his leg in tribute.

Having dutifully christened Italy, Skippy is safely back aboard the *Empire State*. Bob catches the returning launch ashore. It is July 15—his twentieth birthday. He didn't mention it to anybody. What for? It isn't as if they'd bake him a cake. But now he wishes he had told someone. Groups of cadets are scattered here and there on the square, following guides, negotiating prices with gondoliers. Bob wishes he could join them. He strolls the square, flying squads of pigeons swooping this way and that.

Just off the square, he happens upon Harry's Bar—famous from Hemingway. Bob gazes through the window, around the bar's name, frosted into the glass in large letters. It's small inside—just four stools at the bar. On one of them is Jerry Doyle, perched like a fireplug, his bowed legs spread wide. Doyle is holding up his glass and pointing to it and heatedly explaining something to the bartender. Bob opens the door.

". . . brown a shade not much found in martinis." Doyle is saying.

The bartender, olive-skinned, slicked back hair, young, looks darkly at him. "Yew ast for 'a mahrteeny wis rye,' " he says, emphatically.

"I said 'a martini dry'!" Doyle bellows. "That tasted like a lollipop. Dry, not rye. Dry! Dry! Jesus Christ God Almighty, can't you people do anything?" The bartender stares at him, motionless. "Oh, for hell's sake, just pour me a glass of gin, will ya?" says Doyle. The bartender, never taking his eyes off Doyle, slowly moves his hands to his task.

Bob smiles and sits down. "Hello, Jerry," he says.

"SPARKS!" Jerry shouts, grabbing Bob by the neck and giving him a few hard shakes. Doyle lets go, taps out something—a complex series of raps on the bar, using two fingers from each hand. *Brap-apap-pap-pap, braaaap, pap, pap pap pap, bappity pap.*

"Wass that?" he says, doing it again. Bob listens, smiling and shaking his head back and forth. "Awww, never mind," Doyle says. "Have a drink. Tony, give this man a drink."

"Wart well you haff, sehr?" says the bartender, whose name tag reads "Alberto."

"A gin fizz," says Bob. He looks around Harry's, settling in. "It's a lot smaller than I expected. Where's Hemingway?"

"Haven't seen 'im," says Doyle. "But I'm ready."

"Ready?"

Doyle sits up very straight on his stool, squares his powerful shoulders, holds up his glass of iced gin at arm's length, and looks skyward, as if making a toast. " 'The worrrrrld is a fine place and worrrrth the *fightin'* for,' " he says, smiling at Bob, immensely proud, rewarding himself with a long sip of his drink. "That's Hemingway."

"It is?"

"It is. I think it is. Anyway, he'll know whether it is or not. But he hasn't been around, Tony says, in years."

"Maybe tonight will be the night he comes back," says Bob.

"Mebbe," says Doyle. The bartender sets a drink before Bob, who reaches down for it, and the evening compresses into memory. A long, intense discussion of the pros and cons of the Olivetian universe, Doyle's discovery of Bob's birthday. Toasts. Many, many gin fizzes. A plate of very expensive spaghetti somewhere. Another bar. Doyle delivering some sort of intense advice, his face very close to Bob's, poking his finger hard against Bob's chest.

St. Mark's Place is dark and deserted by the time they head back for the midnight running boat to the ship. The last boat. Crossing the square, Jerry rolling lopsidedly on his barely functional legs, Bob abruptly stops, catching sight of the *Empire State*, all lit up, neatly framed between the pillars, the covered gondolas at the pier bobbing rapidly up and down at the water's edge. As if he had never seen the ship before and is seeing her for the first time. "Man," he whispers to himself.

"Come on, we'll mish it," says Doyle, tugging at his arm, and they hurry to the boat landing. The next morning they leave for Greece.

Steaming out of Venice, the *Empire State II* passes the British Mediterranean Fleet. Bob has already been thinking about the ships sent to the bottom during the war—ghostly twisted hulls passing silently underneath. And now, to have this armada—destroyers, battleships, an aircraft carrier—loom on the horizon and pass to starboard. Well, it's just too much.

But that's only a taste of what is to come. A few days later, shortly after the *Empire State* anchors in the harbor at Piraeus, the port of Athens, the U.S. Sixth Fleet steams in, its air wing just *screaming* by overhead, so low you find yourself ducking, involuntarily.

As if that isn't thrill enough, as if the needle weren't already pinned, the commander of the fleet is away on official business, making the president of the State University of New York Maritime College, Vice-Admiral Calvin T. Durgin, USN (Ret.), who boarded the ship in Venice, and whose cabin is next to Bob's, the ranking officer for United States naval forces in the Mediterranean.

The *Empire State* moves down the line of Navy vessels to take on fuel from a fleet oiler, and the summer sailors and green cadets and aging instructors line the rail, puffed with pride as, one by one, the ships in the fleet acknowledge the vice-admiral's flag flying from the mast of the scrappy little former assault transport ship, a load of pig iron bolted in her belly.

That's the high. The low comes swiftly enough. The next day a Brazilian ship, *El Mirante Saldanha,* moors across from the *Empire State* and somehow drops her anchor right on top of the *Empire State*'s anchor. The two chains tangle. Captain Olivet is livid. The navigator, Guy DeSimone, has to actually hold him back; he seems about to crawl over the rail, dive into the harbor, swim to the *El Mirante Saldanha,* and murder her captain.

Disentanglement is a lengthy, unpleasant, ungraceful procedure conducted in full sight of the Sixth Fleet, involving much careful maneuvering back and forth at one-eighth speed and much screaming over the radiotelephone in English and Portuguese. The vice-admiral's flag hangs limply from the staff above the bridge, as if mocking them.

At the embassy party in Athens, Bob dances almost every dance with the wife of the captain of an American destroyer based there, a captain called away to Belgium for a meeting. She is flirtatious and Southern—from Mississippi, like Jan Anderson.

"Why don't you stop by my apartment for tea on Sunday?" she asks, brushing a sweaty strand of hair away from her face after a dance.

"I can't," Bob says. "We sail on Sunday."

"Saturday, then," she replies, fixing him a look. Bob hears himself say he will, borrowing a pencil to take down her address on the back of a napkin.

If they left for the apartment right then, that might have been one thing. But the day's delay gives Bob a chance to brood. A married woman. The wife of a captain. What is he getting himself into? Trouble is what.

Still, he is human. He leaves the ship on Saturday morning looking his best. It is a long train trip from Piraeus to Athens and it gives him time to think. Instead of heading for the address, he finds himself wandering around Athens, ending up in an open-air market, staring at the flies crawling over cuts of meat hanging from the stalls. He locates a phone and calls the destroyer captain's wife: I'm sorry, he says, but I can't make it to tea.

The next day they sail for France. In Villefranche sur Mer they have a celebration called White Night. Bands are playing, people are singing, yelling. Not knowing French the way he knows Spanish, the scene is even more disorienting and dreamlike for Bob, a whirl of parades and songs and shouts and fireworks. Walking Skippy, he hooks up somehow with a short-haired woman in toreador pants walking a Pomeranian, and they end up, arm in arm in a procession of some sorts, Bob wearing his officer's hat turned backward.

These people know how to live. But Bob doesn't, apparently, and—the woman with the little dog notwithstanding—most French strangers can somehow tell on sight. At the welcoming party Bob is among a group of officers when he notices an exotic French woman in an iridescent green sleeveless summer dress, looking hard at him over the rim of her cocktail. He straightens up and smiles at her. She walks over to the group and speaks, not to him, but to John Arkinstall.

"How eeze eet," she says, with a cool nod of the head toward Bob, "zet yew haff offisays who ahr sisteen yehrs old?"

* * *

The night the ship leaves Villefranche, Bob goes to bed early. About 2 o'clock in the morning a warning buzzer rips him awake.

"General quarters. General quarters," says a voice over the speaker. "Fire on the mess deck. Fire on the mess deck. All hands on the double."

Fire? Bob leaps out of bed and the ship pitches, projecting him into a wall. A storm. The deck is pitching like mad. And a fire. He steadies himself, switches on the light, jumps into his pants, sitting back hard onto his bunk, luckily, when the ship gives a sharp pitch. He hurries to the mess deck, in his life jacket, his heart pounding like a rabbit's.

The mess deck is chaos, but no fire. There's glass everywhere, and what looks like a big fan, smashed. DeSimone clues him in—they hit rough seas in the channel coming out of Villefranche. The fan broke loose, taking a table and a glass ashtray with it. Commander Maley called for twenty cadets to come clean it up and, after half an hour, only two showed. So he got mad and sounded general quarters. That brought them running.

What a crew, Bob thinks, heading back to his bunk. *I can't wait to get off this ship.*

From France, back to Spain. Valencia is hot, hotter than Majorca. The last port before heading home. Bob sits by the pool at El Club Nautico. An old *duenna* comes over, fingers the Star of David he wears around his neck on a chain, and says *"lansman"*—Yiddish for "kinsman"—and fishes out her own star from beneath layers of black.

That is how he meets Maria Rodriguez Teressa Cono, the Catholic teenager in the care of the Jewish *duenna*.

Maria Teressa invites him home to dinner. He goes, later that night, in a horse-drawn cab. The dining room is dark, with a long, medieval refectory table covered in a lace tablecloth. Bob must, the father says, be uncomfortable in his dress uniform in this heat.

"Hace caliente," Bob says, running a finger along his collar. The father insists that Bob go into his bedroom and change into his pajamas. The pajamas are silk, finely made, sky blue with dark piping, monogrammed, clean. Bob hesitates, looking around the room and its large, mahogany furniture—dresser, draped in lace, armoire, a chair for a king, carved wood with a red velvet seat. He puts the pajamas on nervously, glancing at the door, keeping on his underwear, leaving his uniform folded carefully on the bed. He steps into slippers and returns to the dining room.

Maria sits to his right. Her father sits to his left. Standing behind him is Maria's older sister, holding a large rattan fan on a stick. As soon as he sits down, she starts to fan him. Bob can't believe it. He tries to protest. "This is not required." But they wave him off.

Her father, the minister of agriculture in Valencia, speaks no English. He seems to be asking about American crops. Bob tells him what he knows, which was almost nothing, struggling for Spanish for corn, feeling the fan go behind him, the candlelight twinkling through the heavy cut glass of the wine goblet.

How, he wonders, how am I ever going to go back to Ohio State after this? How am I going to get in the cafeteria line? Ride the bus? They will never believe it. Never in a million years.

Maria's family clusters around the dining room table. Everyone is very formal, but very friendly. Bob can't look anyone in the face without getting a big, sincere smile in return. Bob doesn't even know how to smile that broadly. He feels wrong doing it, like he is leering, or grimacing, or showing too many teeth.

Bob can't help but think back to his own family at dinner: his father silently reading the newspaper, oblivious to all of them. His mother, never sitting down, placing the food wordlessly on the table, observing closely to provide material for future criticisms. His brother, wolfing back the brisket, chewing with his mouth open. The click of the silverware.

Maria has short hair, a wonderful accent. Cheerful, sympathetic. She is sixteen years old. The second night they sit at a table in a nightclub, the *duenna* perched on a chair a few feet away, facing them placidly. Maria asks about Bob's "intentions."

Bob thinks a long time. "I'm Jewish," he says. "You're Catholic. We can't have intentions."

Maria's smile doesn't dim. She draws with her finger on the tablecloth. Here is God, she says, making a small circle. Then a short line straight down, where she makes a little cross. "And here is Jesus." She taps the spot. "Now," she says. A short line to the left. "Here are the Catholics." A short line to the right. "And here are the Jews."

"You see?" she says, her beautiful black eyes sparkling. "It is all the same."

Bob hates the world back home. He sees what is in store for his friends, for him. And this new world is so intriguing. Everyone here seems so nice. And they have servants. He is not a particularly devout Jew. But still; it is not all the same. It is not the same.

"Non," he says. With his left hand, he taps the spot where God is, follows it down to Jesus, then over to the Catholics. Then, with his right, he taps the Jews, and shoots the line straight up to God, with no Jesus involved.

They will write to each other for a year. He will keep the bottle of port she signs for the rest of his life. But eventually the letters will stop and they will never see each other again.

Bob and the other officers head to a bullfight. Unlike at a ballpark, at a bull ring the best seats—the governor's box, for instance—are up top, farthest away from the action. The officers sit down low, near the ground. Everyone is feeling in a good mood, gay from the sangria at lunch, their hearts swelling with the enormous shouts of the crowd. *"OLÉ!"* A victorious matador struts over to their box and bows low. Commander Maley breaks off from clapping to fish into his pocket. He draws out two fresh packs of Lucky Strikes. As executive officer, he has an endless supply. He happily tosses the cigarettes down to the matador. They land at his feet, in the dirt, among the roses, and the matador looks down at them, then up at the box of officers. In Bob's mind, the stadium falls silent. The matador gives the officers a steady, level stare of burning hatred, for a long time, as if memorizing their faces, then turns abruptly and walks away. The Lucky Strikes remain where Maley has tossed them, trampled by hooves, for the rest of the bullfight, which suddenly loses its savor for the officers, who soon depart.

The next morning the *Empire State* sets sail for New York.

Bob writes to his mother from Valencia and tells her to bring a tanker truck of milk to the pier. He loves milk and hasn't had any since leaving New York, two and a half months earlier. He can't drink the milk on the ship (powdered) nor in port (unhomogenized).

The crossing back over the Atlantic sinks into increasingly dreary routine. The individual bad qualities each crew member has been suppressing are now not suppressed so tightly. Men snarl at each other in passing. And just when it seems that nothing will happen—three days from home—something does. The doctor of the *Empire State* kills the captain of another ship.

Well, maybe not *kills*, though the less charitable officers view it that way. A sleepy Sunday afternoon. Late August at sea. At 8 A.M.—the beginning of Bob's morning shift—he slips into the radio room. Powers up the console. Flips off the auto-alarm and turns the volume up on the speaker. Over the ship's intercom a voice squawks: "Sweepers, man your brooms, clean sweep down fore and aft." Bob savors momentary pleasure at never having to touch a broom.

A quarter after—the minute hand creeps into the red pie-shaped zone on the clock, time to monitor the distress frequency. Bob tunes in to 500 kilocycles. He listens for the required three minutes, and is about to turn it down and jot the customary note in the log— "Silence," when the speaker erupts: *dit dit dit, dah dah dah, dit dit dit. . . .*

It repeats three times, just long enough for Bob to snap forward in his chair and flop his fingers onto the typewriter keys. No problem understanding that message: SOS, SOS, SOS—FROM LMJE— S.S. CORO—CAPTAIN HEART ATTACK—ANY SHIP WITH DOCTOR—PLEASE HELP—SOS, SOS, SOS, POSITION—LAT 38.22.5 N.—LONG. 30.37.3 W.

Bob listens to the static. He clamps the headphones over his ears so he can hear better. Half a minute passes. *Where the hell is everybody? We can't be the only ship around.* Then the *Coro* starts up the message again: *dit dit dit, dah dah dah, dit dit dit. . . .*

That snaps Bob out of his stunned stupor. He grabs the Vibroplex and signals back, hard, leaning forward, caught in the moment: LMJE, LMJE—FROM KGWE. T.S. EMPIRE STATE—COPY YOUR S.O.S. WE HAVE DOC. PLEASE CONFIRM YOUR POSITION— 38.22.5 N, 30.37.3 W.

—FROM LMJE—CONFIRMED.

—LMJE FROM KGWE—OK—STANDBY.

Bob yanks the paper out of the typewriter and runs through the chartroom to the bridge. Guy DeSimone takes a pair of calipers and plots the *Coro*'s position on the chart. "Looks like we're it," he says to the captain, who tells Bob to let them know they're on their way—the ships are seventy-five miles apart, a three-hour trip, if they don't miss each other in the ocean's vastness.

Bob is in the radio room tapping out a message to the *Coro* when he feels someone standing behind him—John Arkinstall.

"Can you handle things, Bob, or do you want me to take over?" Bob waves him away. "I'm fine, thanks." Mr. Arkinstall reminds Bob to move up to 535 kilocycles; he's still on the 500 kilocycle emergency frequency. "Yeah, right, thanks," Bob says.

Mr. Arkinstall lingers for a moment, then goes up to the bridge to man the radio direction finder—it'll help locate the *Coro* as the ships approach each other.

The two ships take five hours to meet. Finally the lookout on the *Empire State* spots the *Coro*—a decrepit tanker sailing under the Liberian flag.

The *Empire State* has a doctor, of sorts. He is a Park Avenue gynecologist enjoying a summer cruise, a fact that provides an endless source of merriment. Down below in the engine room Jerry Doyle hears that the *Empire State* is slowing to send a running boat with the doctor to another ship to aid her captain. "Is he having a baby?" Doyle asks.

The seas are choppy. The doctor and his son—a third-year medical student along for the ride—neither looking very happy, manage to get into the motor launch. It peels away and races over to the *Coro*, piloted by First Mate Fred Bidgood. Two hours later the doctor returns, "He'll be fine," the doctor says, exuding calm and authority. "He's resting comfortably in his quarters. I told them they better get back to the Azores." The next morning Bob receives a message from the *Coro*, relayed through Chatham Radio: "KGWE, KGWE: EMPIRE STATE THANK YOU FOR ASSISTING; CAPTAIN DIED IN NIGHT. LMJE, CORO."

Later, Bob finds out the doctor's son isn't really a third-year medical student, but a first-year optometry student. *Christ*, he thinks, *I wonder if his dad is even a gynecologist.*

* * *

Then New York. The agony of anchoring for twenty-four hours off City Island, with Manhattan in sight, waiting for the next morning, so that the *Empire State* can sail in on schedule, flags aflutter. The last night on the ship Bob stands at the rail, mesmerized by the glittering skyline, brighter than the stars, wondering what it all meant—the past three months, Conchita and Maria and the rest. He decides he'll figure it out later.

That night the captain has a farewell party for the officers in the outer room of his quarters. Captain Olivet sits in the middle of the gathering, unsmiling, eyes drilling fiercely into the face of whoever is brave enough to talk to him. Bob takes his drink and drifts over to Jack Sklaar.

"Are you coming back next year, Bob?" Sklaar asks.

"Sure," says Bob. "I think so."

"I hope so," says Sklaar. "You're the best second-radio officer we've had in a long time."

Probably the only one you've had, Bob thinks, searching for the dark in every silvered cloud. *The only one who didn't have to be carried aboard every night the ship sat in port.*

The next day makes the entire three-month journey worthwhile. In June, the *Empire State* had snuck out the back door, through Long Island Sound. In August, she returns triumphantly through the glorious front gate of New York Harbor, past the Statue of Liberty and a pair of city fireboats, spouting their greetings and whirring their sirens. Then up the East River to Fort Schuyler, where a thousand people wait.

Bob is in the radio shack until the last moment, hurriedly copying out greetings from ships in the harbor, glancing when he can through the open door at the sights. Suddenly Mr. Arkinstall appears in the doorway. "You can go watch, Bob," he says.

"Are you sure?" Bob asks. "It's my shift."

"I'm sure," says Arkinstall, who first boarded the *Empire State* in 1930, when she still had sails. "I've seen it before."

Bob thanks him. Mr. Arkinstall shakes his hand and says that he hopes he'll see him back next year. Bob says he's sure he will, then he hurries out to join the men leaning over the rail, waving their hats over their heads waiting for the fort to come into view.

Bob has drawn his final pay: $600. The purser only has singles left—or so he said—and handed Bob six bundles of 100 singles. He has them jammed in every pocket.

Bob looks at the liners tied up at the famous piers. He thinks back to the day—just five years ago?—when he had his parents drive him down to the docks. He wanted to go aboard the S.S. *America* and see her radio room. But he lost his nerve at the sight of the great ship, and instead went aboard a smaller Italian liner at the next berth. Through hand signals—a pantomime finger tapping—he made it understood he wanted the radio room. The operator, a small dark man with a mustache, eating his lunch, paused to point to the dials and then, just as Bob was leaving, with a wink handed him a girlie pin-up poster. Bob was embarrassed but stuffed it under his shirt and hurried back to his parents on the pier.

And now he is *on* a ship, his ship, finishing his first cruise to Europe. Bob scans the city, the streets and windows of the apartment buildings passing swiftly by, searching for a little boy's face, a face slack with wonder and unformed hope. Searching for himself.

They arrive at Fort Schuyler. Olivet sets the ship against the pier with a thud. The cadet band on deck launches into "Columbia, the Gem of the Ocean." The lines are cast and secured. The ship's horn toots a long, last blast before the boilers are shut down. Captain Olivet issues his final order of the summer: dismiss the crew. Duffel bag over his shoulder, Bobby joins the logjam of sailors pressing to get off the ship. Smiling broadly, anticipating the joyful reunion, he strides down the gangplank, only a little afraid no one will be there to meet him. He takes a few steps, looks around, buffeted by the swirl of people. Nobody. Nobody. Nobody. Then he hears his name shouted, and sees his family—father, mother, brother. Bobby grins broadly. His mother takes one look at him and bursts into tears. He has lost thirty pounds.

"Jack Armstrong, the All-American Boy!" Morty shouts, slapping him on the back. "Look at you! Skin and bones!" He runs his fingers down Bobby's ribs, then gives him a hard punch in the shoulder and a harder hug. His father, smiling broadly, hooks an arm around his neck and pulls Bobby toward him, giving him an inexpert kiss on the side of the head. His mother, hanging on his arm, says, "I've got everything at home—chicken, potato pudding, noodle kugal, and milk—a half gallon of milk!" Together, arm in arm, they walk toward the car, through the commotion of hugging and kissing and shouting. The scene freezes: Sam wearing Bobby's hat backward; Bobby with one arm over his father's shoulders, one over his mother's; his brother Morty a step in front of them, holding Bobby's sea bag in one arm, turning to make a sweeping gesture with the other as he says something funny. Then the image disappears, like dust puffed off a mantel, and we are back in the present again.

BOOK THREE

Homeward Bound

This, let me remind you again, is a love story;
you can see it by the imbecility.
—JOSEPH CONRAD, *LORD JIM*

We started at the beginning—his earliest memories, in the crib in the Bronx, the breeze blowing in from the air shaft. He sat on his bunk; I sat tipped back in the plastic chair.

No matter where we began, however, we always came back to the same terrible place, to a sense of sadness, of loss, the same peevish family squabbles—his father's stamp collection, with its beautiful zeppelins and winged globes, sold quickly by Morty after their father's death to finance his son Jeffrey's crass circus-like bar mitzvah. My dad's love-hate for his father, his collapsing on the street in New York, a scene I thought of so much it was as if it had happened to me. The Long Fall. I picture it in slow motion, in fatal silence, the normal city streetscape suddenly skewing, the horizon going vertical. The monster's fist closing around his heart and twisting. The grotesque gray ovals of a few strangers' faces, inches away, mouths moving silently. The white slap of death.

"I did not want to be like my father, I had no father," my father said. "Of course I did love him. When I saw him in the casket, I kissed him on the forehead, I always thought I did not want to be like my father."

CHAPTER 8

The Sea's Outcry

The Atlantic Ocean is exactly half the size of the Pacific. A cubic foot of seawater weighs sixty-four pounds; of ice, fifty-six pounds. After oxygen and nitrogen, the most common element in air is argon—nearly a full percent. For every nautical mile a ship travels, the earth curves downward 9.6 inches.

We were out at sea now. The navigator, John Ryan, gave me a copy of Bowditch's *The American Practical Navigator*, an 850-page tome that, in various editions, has been helping sailors cross the ocean for nearly two hundred years. I plunged into it, captivated.

Fog was defined in a 243-word epic beginning, "A visible accumulation of tiny droplets of water" and touching upon sea fog, ice fog, true fog, and mock fog, among others, before segueing into related fog phenomena, such as the faint circular arc of color sometimes glimpsed in fog and called, wonderfully, a "fogbow."

It was enough to keep me happy for days. I loved knowing that a square foot is 0.000022957 acres. I couldn't imagine how that helps a ship get from point A to point B, but it was there in the book, so it must be useful, somehow.

The book inspired me to try to learn celestial navigation. I sat in on Hap Parnham's class, and went to the flying bridge to watch the cadets shoot the stars. They used a sextant—a 250-year-old optical instrument with a small telescope to look at the horizon. Turning a knob, the horizon is brought, via a mirror, to just touch a star, or planet, or the sun, and that way determines the latitude of a ship, with the help of an almanac and lengthy calculations.

The ship's roll is most pronounced on the flying bridge, a small outdoor area, cluttered with antennae, directly above the bridge. At sunset, a dozen cadets gathered, each holding a sextant, each facing a different direction, buffeted by the wind, some standing, legs braced wide, some kneeling, trying not to be in each other's line of sight. One of the cadets let me use his sextant. I shot Mars, Spica, and Venus, then met the cadet later to do the calculations, which involved tables and adjustments for atmospheric reflections and other factors. One of the variables, I was impressed to note, is the height of the observer. In making a triangle using yourself, the horizon, and a star, it matters whether you are five feet or six feet off the deck of the ship. That seemed reassuring, a glimmer of cosmic significance.

We would be at sea for a solid week before reaching the coast of Africa. I settled into a routine, teaching, writing columns, exercising in the weight room. Every Tuesday was a tedious, hour-long lifeboat drill, where we all assembled on the deck and stood around, gazing into space, ruminating on the possibility of shipwreck and waiting for our names to be called. Then there were papers to grade and student crises to iron out. It seemed I was always hurrying from one part of the ship to another, my head turned sharply to the side, studying the ocean. I never tired of looking at its vastness, occasionally in my mind superimposing dozens of downtown Chicagos over the horizon, to marvel at just how big the ocean is, a blue emptiness stretching in all directions.

And my father? He seemed visibly unhappy. Everyone commented on it. They didn't say, "Your father seems visibly unhappy." What they said was, after asking me how I was doing and hearing a positive report, "And is your father having a good time?" They all used that exact phrase, as if reading it off a cue card.

But when I challenged him on it, he denied anything was wrong. I didn't believe him, but I let it go. Our exchanges had begun to resemble a Beckett play. My father was striding around the room, stretching, doing inclined push-ups against the desk.

"Do you find that you're bothered by this motion a lot?" he asked.

"No," I said, not looking up from my book.

He grabbed an orange from the basket of fruit he had taken back from the mess and began to peel.

"That smell of the orange doesn't bother you?" he said.

"No."

"I thought I'd have some."

"I said I liked it the other day."

"I thought you were trying to be nice or something."

"No. Go ahead."

"Would you like some?" he said, offering a slice.

"No," I said, looking up from the book. "Thank-you."

The captain suggested that my dad teach a special class, like Parnham's seminar on celestial navigation. I passed the suggestion along, adding a few words of encouragement, even though I of course worried what kind of Captain Queeg-like breakdown he would have in front of an audience. I figured the risk would be worth it if he could spend a day or two lost in the preparation of a lecture.

And he did give it thought; first something on natural selection, then a sweeping indictment of the lack of weather charts on the ship. But in the end he let the idea drop.

*   *   *

The weather charts were his new concern. Warnings are sent by the weather service, but conditions aren't plotted out.

"When I was on the *Empire State* they had a big chart with the entire route mapped on it, all the way to Europe," he said, as if he weren't on the ship now. "Here they have a blank chart with a line on it. Big deal. They don't know where the highs and lows are. They don't know where they are. I don't want to be negative. I don't want to say I'm an expert. Maybe the captain has charts back in his room."

At least we communicated, we talked about things that bothered us, usually as they were happening. I had one of those Plexiglas box frames, with seven photos of my family—I had been unable to settle on a single shot—and I rotated to a new one every day, first thing in the morning, excited to reveal a new scene. That day there was a picture of Kent and Ross treating each other with a toy doctor's bag.

"New picture?" my father said.

"The doctor and his patient," I said.

"Watch the guy on the right. The real chief. Watch the guy on the right. A tough cookie."

It was a neutral statement, but his "real chief" comment resonated with past things he had said, always something about my boys manipulating me. That was an unspoken belief of my father's: people didn't have emotions, opinions, feelings—not genuine ones. Rather, they had ersatz emotions, opinions, and feelings they use to control others. There was a line from a Karl Shapiro poem—"As the young, detecting an advantage, practice a face"—he loved to quote so often that I could feel my jaw tense every time he said it.

We approached the Canary Islands. I was surprised at how quickly. On the third day out of Bridgetown, the captain had the charts out in the ward room.

At dinner, the librarian, Mr. Folcarelli, asked me if I knew what the Canary Islands were named for.

"Ummm . . . canaries?" I ventured.

"No, dogs," he said. "From the Latin for "dog," *caninus.* They discovered birds there, later, and named them for the island."

A marvelous world.

After class, I returned to my cabin and found Dad spread across his bed, a wet rag covering his face.

"You know what I'm going to miss?" he said, popping up and pulling off the rag. "You don't get grease coming out of your face in Colorado. At the end of the day here your face is like a grease ball."

"That's the romance of the sea, Dad," I said. It was the first time he said he was going to miss something about the trip.

We locked the door and poured the rum. Liquor was forbidden on the ship, but we couldn't have been the only ones drinking in our room. My father had noted, several times, that certain officers were always scurrying out to scoop big pitchers of ice from the machine and disappearing into their rooms. I wondered if anybody noticed that I was filling two cups with ice every night about 9 P.M.

These evening conversations always were more pleasant than our morning talks. We spoke of the past, his trips, his growing up, a little about us kids. I had thought that my father would be a font of memories about us when we were little, but the cupboard was bare, with only a few dry crumbs scattered around. He remembered that I was smart and Debbie troubled. Just as he was going over, again, the old problems of my sister, I interrupted him, asking if he had any *happy* memories of Debbie.

The question seemed to startle him. "When she was eight years old," he said. A pause. Then silence. That was it.

"And what?" I asked.

"And we went to buy her a watch in downtown Berea," he said, quickly, dismissively, as if he were just grabbing at anything.

The subject was dropped. We sipped our rum.

Captain Ahlstrom took me on a tour of the ship. He knew every gauge, it seemed. Down in the keel was shaft alley, the drive shaft that connected the engine to the propeller. The girth of a telephone pole, the shaft ran the length of the ship from the engine to the stern. It spun briskly, but slow enough that you could pat it with your palm, and I did. The surface was mottled with rust. I asked the captain why.

"They used to keep it polished," he said. "Captain DeSimone had cadets holding emery clothes to it while it spun. I didn't think it was worth the risk of a cadet mangling his hand."

That seemed a very modern concern, something they would have never thought about in the good old days when decorum dictated that the shaft be kept shiny.

The rusty shaft seemed a symbol of the divergence between the old and new ways. Keeping the shaft polished was not an entirely meaning-less activity—it certainly would look better than the rusty shaft. But it was cosmetic; that solid steel shaft wouldn't rust through in a hundred years, and somebody could, conceivably, get his or her hand chewed up. Maybe that's worth the risk, if the sight of a rusty shaft makes you think the world's sliding to hell. Maybe not.

A number of officers made a point of taking me aside to complain about the school. Standards were being lowered. Subpar cadets were admitted. But I wasn't really interested in the internal politics of the Maritime College; academic life is generally ruined by power plays and pissing matches. I was interested in how the shaft passed through the hull of the ship to turn the four-bladed, nickel-aluminum-bronze alloy propeller. What sealed the opening? It turns out that the shaft is col-lared by wood: lignum vitae, a dense, oily wood that lubricates itself. The last vestige of wooden ships, hidden within all that steel.

That night, over our snootful of rum, my father and I felt good, and we toasted our trip. Dad told me not to worry about Naples— everything would work out fine. His way of venting his concerns was to out-of-the-blue reassure me. He was intensely afraid of Naples, very concerned about where the ship would dock and how long a walk it would be to the end of the pier. "Go to Naples and die," was a catch phrase my father had dredged up from his cruise days. And in fact, the Fort Schuyler yearbook, *Eight Bells,* for 1953 noted of Naples, "We toured the city in groups of four or more—to walk alone at night is suicide."

We planned to spend the first night in port on the ship to get our feel for the country before catching a train to Rome. I offered to go to the train station myself the day we docked and get the train tickets, so he wouldn't have to worry.

"No way," he said. "I'll go with you." He would watch my back.

I wasn't nearly as concerned. Then again, I had a secret smattering of Italian. The six weeks before we got on the ship I had taken a two-hour Italian class every Tuesday evening at the Latin School, Chicago's posh private academy. I didn't tell my father. It was going to be a surprise. Cornered in some difficult situation in Naples, I'd look coolly at my father, register the panic in his eyes, pause just a moment, then, a slight smile playing about my lips, reel off a few choice phrases in melodious Italian, amazing him and the locals. As the ruffians backed away, or the haughty waiter was reduced to head-bowed efficiency, my father would gaze at me, astonished. "I learned Italian," I'd say, with a dismissive wave of the hand. "I thought it might come in handy."

That was the plan, anyway. It got off to a good start. The teacher had the lovely name of Giuseppe Dragonetti. A neatly dressed character with a connoisseur's paunch, Dragonetti didn't just press vocabulary and grammar into us, but performed a sort of one-man show that could have been titled, "The Cultured World of Italia vs. American Life Wasted on Ignorant Crap."

He asked us how we pronounce *bruschetta*. The class peppered him with *"bru-shet-ta"*s. Wrong! The *sch* is not slurred, *shhh,* but hard, *sk—bru-sket-ta*. We should not be embarrassed to say it properly, even if everyone who hears us thinks it is we who are mistaken. "It's okay to be right," he said. "Why would you perpetrate stupid mistakes?"

Dragonetti solemnly outlined Italian habits as if they were eternal truths. "Forget about the big spoon," he said. "That is an American invention. Do not eat pasta with a spoon in Italy, period. Do not put parmesan cheese on your seafood. Educated people should know." I took careful notes: "No big spoon. No parmesan on seafood."

I was so confident I could somehow master the language in just six weeks, and then retain it after a month across the ocean, that my wife felt duty-bound to mock me. I was reviewing my homework when she leaned close to me, eyes glittering mischievously, and said, in a heavy, foreign accent: "I vood like . . . to rrrent . . . a feesh." Then she walked away, laughing.

I spent most of the next day in the engine room, going over the mechanics of the ship with Chief Jackson. The captain must have put the word to him because after brushing me off for weeks, he suddenly invited me down to examine the works.

The engine room was complex, but I wanted to try to gain at least a rough understanding of the system. I hated the thought that it couldn't be grasped. That curiosity must in part be due to being the son of a scientist. I'm always writing stories about complex procedures. Most reporters are hot to break news; I'm more excited to write about how a big supermarket works or how a heart is transplanted or steel is made.

To me, there was a freakish beauty to the engine room's weirdly shaped pipes: pipes that rounded out, like pregnant bellies, to direct pressure, but seemed to be actually bulging, as if in a cartoon, about to burst. Huge conduits for seawater, scoop injectors, circulating pumps.

While I was being shown around by Jackson—an open, affable man, with the easygoing nature of someone deeply knowledgeable and certain in his field—my father was up in the radio room, spending hours trying to find WCC Chatham Radio, the old land station he used to transmit messages to and from. It was gone.

Afterward, I stopped by the radio room. Dad was still there, listening intently on the headphones. I almost didn't recognize him at first. In profile, his face looked a little shrunken, older than I thought, his hair more white than black. I stood in the doorway for a while, waiting for him to notice me. His face was set in concentration, the back of one hand pressed against his lips, the other working the dials. He never noticed me, and I left him there.

Sunday barbecue on the aft deck—our third aboard ship. A beautiful day. Backlit clouds, cadets in beach wear, lounging around eating burgers. I felt glad to hear music blasting out of big speakers. I really missed music. Many cadets had brought boom boxes, but I hadn't.

In my fantasy, the students at the barbecue would come over to me, shyly at first, and continue discussions from class, beaming, introducing me to their friends—a real newspaper columnist, right here, in our midst. Nobody said a word. Nobody even looked at me.

That evening my father and I finished our bottle of rum. It was more significant to my dad, because he didn't know there was a spare bottle to take us through the final week at sea. I was saving the news for the right moment of obvious drama. He spoke about Geneva—he used to spend a lot of time there, working for the World Meteorological Organization. Our family lived there one summer at No. 10, Avenue des Amazones. It was exciting for him to work with other agencies, other nations. I had to remind myself that my view of his career as a dud was just my view, a stale leftover from my unattractive, surly teen years. It had to seem thrilling to him. He once brought a Russian scientist—certainly a KGB agent, we all agreed—home for dinner. To Carteret Court in Berea, Ohio. (We must have been right because the FBI felt the need to debrief my father afterward.) It was thrilling. I would have been thrilled, had it been me, riding in the jump seat of a 747 to Europe, behind the pilot. Had it been me the pilot let sit in his chair, before the controls, for half an hour, while he took a rest. The co-pilot had shot my father a stern look as he settled into the seat next to him, and my father said, "I know better than to touch anything." Had it been me, I'd be impressed.

It was late. We finished our rum and called it night.

The next evening I was sitting at the desk in our room, admiring the empty Cockspur bottle, with its strutting rooster. I hadn't been able to throw it away. It seemed to cry out for a proper send-off.

Taking a sheet of yellow legal paper, I wrote:

June 7, '99. Greetings—My name is Neil Steinberg. I am crossing the Atlantic between New York and Naples, by way of Charleston and Barbados, aboard the New York Maritime College Training Ship Empire State.

I am traveling with my father, Robert Steinberg. If you find this message, please write to me describing the circumstances of your discovery. My address is: Neil Steinberg, Chicago Sun-Times, 401 N. Wabash, Chicago, IL 60611. I am a newspaper columnist and writer, 38 years old, married, with two small boys. Thank you for replying.

Then I signed it and went up to the bridge to add our location: "P.S.: My ship's position is, at 8 P.M. the night I put this to sea, N 27:22:77; W 20:10:80 or approaching the Canary Islands."

I rolled the message into a tube and slipped it into the bottle, along with a Barbadian dime. Then I sealed the cap with black electrical tape. I assumed that my father would balk at the project—dumping-at-sea laws, detection by the crew, the Hatch Act, something timid and ridiculous. But he surprised me by enthusiastically joining in the project, picking up the Cockspur bottle with the rolled note inside and admiring it. Would he go with me to pitch it over the side? Sure!

"Better not to premeditate these things," I said, putting on my bulky gray Maritime sweatshirt and tucking the bottle under my right armpit. We went down to the lowest deck and I asked Dad to hold the bottle, for luck. He did, then handed it back to me and I heaved the bottle far out into the rushing wake. It was only then that I noticed a cadet, far down the rail, gazing off into the waters.

My father and I shook hands. "Thanks for coming along," I said. "I wanted to," he said, and I felt abashed at how I assumed he'd be against pitching the bottle.

Back in the room, I speculated on whether anyone would find the message.

"Life is strange that way, you never know," Dad said.

The next day we were due in the Canary Islands.

Very early. Still dark outside, but I could hear people moving about, talking. Something was going on. I was too tired to rise, and lay in bed a while, gathering myself. Finally, I got up and checked my watch: 4:30 A.M. Kneeling on the bed, I pulled back the curtain.

"Shit!" I said, giving the word about three syllables: La Palma, filling the window, it seemed, a steep, cliffed island directly in front of us.

I pulled on clothes and ran to the bridge. The moon was a surprising crescent—hadn't it just been full, a week before? Venus out and bright, the only other object in the royal blue sky. It looked like a stage sky, the crescent moon above a single sparkle of light. The mountains merging into the clouds in the darkness. The ship was steaming at exactly 15 knots.

After about an hour my father joined me, in his khaki baseball hat against the chill of the morning air. "Well, it's Tuesday morning," he said, a joke based on the extraordinary view. We stood there in silence, soaking up the islands after a week at sea.

La Palma must have worn off quickly. Before lunch my father again volunteered how he hadn't wanted to go on the trip, that Mom had to persuade him. He was getting nothing out of it himself; he was doing it as a favor for me. My father said that going back to the Bronx the day before we left New York had been "horrible." The sight of land must have inspired candor. I almost said, "Don't say that, Dad; it doesn't become you." But figured if it was how he felt, why shouldn't he say it? Still, it made me feel low. Leave it to my father to find a way to both go on the trip and negate whatever goodwill his going generated. Sure, I'm spending time with you, but your mother had to struggle for two days to convince me to do it—otherwise I wouldn't have. My time is too precious to waste.

Besides, could I really believe him? Maybe he needed to tell himself that mom had to convince him. For his pride. He couldn't say the trip was important to him, too—couldn't take that risk. I had been with him in the Bronx. He didn't seem to think it was horrible then; he wouldn't leave, kept wanting to go down another street, linger a little longer, to evoke another buried memory.

This is where he had his bar mitzvah. This is the window where his grandmother sat and waited. This is the elementary school. Walking down Pelham Parkway, he had stopped at a corner and said, "This is where the fighter Jake LaMotta killed my friend Alan Berg—he was the only friend I had who lived in a house." That stopped me cold. He had never mentioned *that* before. The details turned out to be less dramatic than the summary. Berg was hit by LaMotta's car, not his fists. But it made me suspect that my father wasn't quite the open book I had thought him to be. And now I saw that maybe his comments on himself weren't the straightforward description that I—in my dull, direct reporter's way—always considered them. They weren't press releases, but a kind of a code that I could crack if I had the key.

I had to practically force him up to the Bronx, and later he couldn't admit that he enjoyed the experience. That would make him nostalgic and he can't be that. Just as, having spent hours searching for Chatham Radio, he announced that it was "no big deal" that he couldn't find it.

"It doesn't matter," he said. "It doesn't matter at all."

Maybe men of that era can't let themselves be seen as caring, emotionally, about anything. Too risky. Think of the heroes of my father's generation: the Lone Ranger, Joe DiMaggio, Gary Cooper. They weren't exactly weeping in each other's arms, gushing about their disappointments.

I began to observe my father more closely. Slowly it dawned on me that he was lying in bed a lot. Not even reading. Just lying there, taking his pulse. I stared at him. He noticed me.

"The body has to get used to sea level," he said. I chewed on this. In Colorado, he was always going on about the effect of altitude, but this was a switch. "Because of oxygen overload?" I ventured. Dad saw where I was going and changed course.

"Hard when you go back," he said. "The body becomes more efficient. A process that changes, that's all."

That night we had dinner with Paul, the oceanographer, and Mr. Folcarelli, the librarian. My father made jokes, but I didn't laugh. The others laughed, so it must have been me. My father was starting to get on my nerves; okay, he had taken my nerves and shucked them like corn. Later, in the room, Dad again parsed the situation of my brother Sam, who married a Japanese woman but didn't consult him, while my thoughts were with the bottle in my locker.

"Don't you wish we had bought another bottle?" I said, trolling the bait for him to bite so I could produce the unexpected bottle with the proper dramatic flourish.

"Not at all," my father said. "One was sufficient. I'm glad we didn't bring any more. That is one thing we wouldn't want to have done."

Oh, well. He stepped out of the room, and I broke out the new rum and poured myself a big, warm, comforting slug. But it felt clandestine, so when he returned, I showed off the bottle.

"It's a shame you don't want some," I teased. "Guess that means more for me." He reached for a paper cup.

"This is a trip of reflection," my father said, nursing his rum. He had realized how much time we spent talking about the past—his youth, growing up, the Bronx. And he didn't like it. "I want to be forward-looking," he said. "Why is it men who always live in the past? Women don't do it."

Women don't have the time. Men live in the past because that's typically where their glory lies. I told him he was sitting too much with Mr. Perry, who ground over the same tales again and again, all starring that man of action, part Everyman, part Don Quixote, part Jesus, Mr. John Perry. He was a Zelig, turning up everywhere, trotting alongside MacArthur, bantering with DeGaulle.

"Perry's not going to meet DeGaulle in the future," I said. "It's a way of impressing people, of making them think you're important. Or were important."

"I think if you have an exciting life you don't go back that way, too much," my dad said.

But we don't have exciting lives, I thought. Or do we? What's an exciting life? You have to climb mountains, right? I found whatever I do, as thrilling as it may be while it's happening, turns dull in retrospect. I remembered walking down the street in my neighborhood the summer before. It was late afternoon, and I was heading home from the store, dragging my groceries—something about carrying a sack of groceries that makes a guy feel abject and sad. I passed a boisterous group of men fifteen years younger than myself, laughing and talking and obviously heading out for the evening, unencumbered. And I thought, *How did I dig myself into this rut? Where did I go wrong to live this life where nothing exciting ever happens?*

It was only then, at that moment, grousing to myself, clutching a brown paper bag, that I remembered: the very day before I had rented a chauffeur-driven Lincoln to rendezvous with the Canadian tall ship *True North* at Hammond Harbor, then spent the entire glorious summer day sailing aboard her into Chicago. And got paid to do it. I had stepped over the rail and climbed eighty feet up into the rigging to hang over the topsail yardarm and tie up the sails, my feet curling around a toe rope.

It had been heart-stopping, then. By the next day—twenty-four hours later—it was nearly forgotten. It didn't affect my image of myself at all. Nothing did. It occurred to me that I had a habit of dulling the shine on whatever success I might stumble upon. I couldn't let it boost me up, couldn't afford to, because I was too afraid of the fall back down, of being one of those puffed-up, oblivious fools impressed with themselves. I sneered at John Perry because I was afraid of becoming him. It was a rare insight for me but, having just observed my father's blindness toward his own passions, his denial of what was important to him, I couldn't help but recognize that I was capable of similar myopia. The window into his life was also a mirror reflecting mine.

The next day was my birthday: thirty-nine. My father stepped out of the shower. "This is a special day, but I can't remember why," he said, smiling. "Saint Swabbin's Day? The end of the war? Oh, that's right—happy birthday."

Dad didn't dwell on the subject. "I was going to get up in the night to write something down—a thought—this is just like the old age home," he continued. "Must have been what it was like for my mother . . . a little room. You get up, walk around."

I had already had that thought, watching my father staring off into space for hours. This was what it would be like for him in a home. Yet I wasn't about to agree. I pointed out that everything he did in Boulder—write, read, paint—he could do here, had he chosen to.

"Oh, no, no," he said immediately. "At home I could call somebody up. Get in the car and drive to the library. And the rolling. The rolling keeps me from accomplishing anything."

The ship was as stable as the floor of a cave. Captain Ahlstrom was good to his reputation as a blue-water captain. After those first two difficult nights, the ride had been smooth. The biggest disappointment of the trip, for me, was our placid crossing. You barely knew you were at sea. No dramatic storms outside of the imagination, no boxcars of swirling green water smashing over the bow.

We had breakfast with the doctor. Dad was still trying to work through his fear of Naples. For the past several days he had fixated on the pier. How far down would we dock? How far would we have to tote our luggage? How many steps through the gauntlet of danger would we be forced to walk? In the library he consulted detailed maps of Naples harbor.

Again, I just couldn't understand his thinking. The ship would dock somewhere—nobody was asking our input on the matter. Wherever it docked, we would walk from there. Three times: once into Naples, the day we arrived, to get our train tickets; once back; then the next morning we would leave for the train station. My father wouldn't even permit us to go to Pompeii, which, being twenty minutes away, I thought we might take the opportunity to see. I tried arguing, but he spiked the idea—too risky—and, as in Barbados, I didn't press the matter.

The doctor, of course, was nonplussed.

"They'll just take your money," he said, soothingly. "They won't kill you."

I had been looking forward to the Strait of Gibraltar as an obvious dramatic highlight—the famous Pillars of Hercules, the Rock of Gibraltar, immortalized in all those insurance ads, and, of course, classical literature. But there was a haze that day, and as we hugged the Moroccan coast—the channel between the two continents is narrow, so ships keep to the right, like cars on a street. We never actually saw the north coast, never saw the Rock. We did see the coast of Morocco, with its high-rise condominiums and beachfront hotels. It looked like every other coastal city in the world. Not a camel or a tent in sight.

Still, I spent a few hours on the bridge. The weather was hazy and brisk. My father came up for a while, and I observed him observing. He seemed edgy, furtive, glancing this way and that, turning about suddenly, leaning back, his feet planted, to examine something, then snapping forward to look at something else, his hands jammed the entire time in his pockets.

Noting this, I slowly withdrew my hands from my pockets, remembering a poem by Leonard Nathan called "My Kind":

> *Memory is a tiny room lit*
> *by a wan lamp. The radio plays*
> *soft static but no one minds.*
>
> *Father yawns. Mother yawns, too,*
> *but hides it behind a hand. I knew*
> *already I was not their child.*
>
> *My kind never yawned. Alert, we waited*
> *for our time (and wait still).*
> *I yawn, thinking about it.*

The end of the voyage loomed. My relief was mingled with a kind of panic. Whatever I had hoped would happen with my father had not happened. Whatever revelation I might have secretly yearned for—despite my surface scoffing at the idea—had not occurred.

The ironic thing is, I had decades of experience failing to connect with my father. Years earlier, when my brother moved back home, briefly, I urged him: "If you're not going to be happy until he stands up and claps, it's going to be a long wait." It was so clear when I was giving advice to Sam. But it was hard to take, myself.

Someone was whistling in the corridor. It couldn't be my father because my father was not a whistler. But it *was* him, returning from working out. We were on different schedules now, no longer doing everything together. I had left for breakfast while he was dressing, and for lack of a better place, sat with Mr. Perry and Gus. My father joined us just as I was finishing.

A glob of grapefruit had been stuck on the tip of Mr. Perry's nose. I certainly wasn't going to tell him, and neither was Gus or my father. I had watched Perry prating on, puffing himself, oblivious to the citrus. One of the indignities of age, I thought, excusing myself.

Half an hour later, my dad came back to the cabin whistling, and collapsed with laughter against the wall. "I'm a child at heart," he gasped. The grapefruit on Mr. Perry's nose—it was the funniest thing in the world to him. "I wasn't going to mention it; I figured Gus would mention it." he said.

Dad was laughing hard, tears welling in his eyes. A short time later he was his old self again. He ran into an instructor he had befriended, Captain Mike, in the hall. Mike asked, jokingly, if I had thrown him out. No, Dad said, he was waiting for the wash and reading Nabokov.

"Nabowho?" Mike said. I thought: so typical of my father. He can't be reading a book—he has to read *Nabokov*. The way his father couldn't go to a resort, he had to go to the *Flagler*. It's like the old Catskills joke: "Help!" the woman shouts running down the beach,

"My son the doctor is drowning!" And the kicker was that Mike didn't know who Nabokov was, or at least pretended not to.

Later, mulling over the episode, I realized that the laughing dad, the kid at heart, broken up over a piece of grapefruit on an old man's nose, was a far more appealing person to me than the guy who was always talking up Darwin and trying to impress people. Perhaps if his father hadn't been such a relentless teaser—almost a tormentor— the happy, joking, relaxed dad would not have been such a rare occurrence.

Dad wasn't relaxed about the future because he feared it; he wasn't comfortable with the past because he regretted it. "I wish I had gone to meet Nabokov in Montreaux," he said, again. "He was there in Switzerland when we were there in 1977."

I knew. I had been the one who told him, noticing that Nabokov died there the summer my dad was working in Geneva. It was a lonely summer for me, a teenager with his family in hidebound Switzerland, despite side trips to such fun spots as Zurich. I spent a lot of time reading—*Dune,* the Hermann Hesse books so popular among teenagers, and as it happened, *Lolita.* I would take the boat to Chillon, just for the ride, to see Byron's castle, reading along the way, eating white chocolate. My father would not have gone to see Nabokov back then if the author had phoned and invited him to tea.

I pointed out to my father—yet again—that Nabokov was on his deathbed that summer. Probably not the best company.

No matter. My father needed to regret things. His father's stamp collection. The van Gogh drawing he saw in Palma was mentioned over and over because he thought he should have bought it from the hotel, as if the hotel would have sold it for what a twenty-year-old ensign could have paid. Even in 1952, a van Gogh was worth something, assuming it was real.

He once told me he could have bought McDonald's stock in the

1960s and we'd all be rich. Technically correct, but overlooking a few vital points. First, he never bought stock of any kind in his life, so the odds of buying McDonald's stock were slim. And second, for years he refused to even allow us to *eat* at McDonald's. He thought it was "a greasy spoon." I clearly remember my mother, yielding to our pleas, stopping at a pay phone to call my father first and ask his permission to go to one of the new red-and-white tile restaurants. To castigate yourself for not buying stock under these circumstances seems pathological. It would be like my viewing the fact that I took a freshman computer programming class at college in 1978 as a lost opportunity to become a Microsoft millionaire, when in fact I hated computer programming, didn't see its utility in life, and wasn't any good at it anyway.

Even his trips to Europe aboard the *Empire State* weren't enough in his mind. He should have jumped ship and joined the expatriate art community in Paris.

"The time was right, the years were right, but I wasn't right," he said. "I was too conservative. I wanted to play a role, observe, and come back. I did not entertain the idea of doing it. I felt like a voyeur. I looked at the scene, I liked what I saw, I didn't stay. What prevented me from going back to Europe for a year? I wasn't a risk taker."

I looked at him thinking: *Why wasn't going on the ship enough?* All your friends are amazed at you—you're the one, in their group, who got away first, got away best, while they were still sitting on benches on Pelham Parkway, gaping at each other. Can't you be happy enough with that?

Directing those thoughts toward him, it dawned on me, very dimly at first, that I could also apply them to myself. Don't regret things. Don't be afraid. Blunder forward blithely. Don't give up the ship. Be proud of your failures, as proud as of your successes. Own them.

Sunday morning, our last day at sea. I lay in bed, wiped out. I was gazing at the low metal ceiling, thinking: a month in a metal room. A month can be an impossibly long time. Usually, the months snap by. Maybe this was worth doing, just to feel the excruciatingly fine fabric of a month. Jim DeSimone, captain of the *Empire State* for ten years and Guy DeSimone's son, later told me that two months aboard the *Empire State* is like a year on a tanker.

My father and I certainly weren't any closer. If anything, we were drawing apart. I caught a whiff of the barbecue. A delicious smoky, saucy smell. Dad came in. "Do you smell charcoal in the room?" he asked, anxiously, as if the place were on fire. "Yes," I said, emphatically. "The barbecue. It smells nice."

He left without a word.

The next morning at 8 A.M. the ship passed Capri, a small mountainous island dipping low in the center and spotted with lovely white homes. My father and I stood on the rail and watched it pass.

After two weeks at sea I was ready to hit land.

From the bridge, Naples did not look threatening. Pink and beige, a citadel of sorts on a hill, a compact city with a Popeye-cartoon-busy port spread out below. A broken-down freighter, so low in the water it didn't seem able to get out of the harbor, never mind reach the sea, slowly inched past. I watched the boat carefully, waiting for the wake of a bigger ship to swamp it.

The cadets heaved to the lines. As we approached, my father bemoaned how far down the pier we were docking. There was a U.S. Navy band waiting where the ship would tie up, but the gangway was causing trouble. A piece of machinery on the dock, a motor winch that lowered the ramp of the pier, kept the gangway from swinging out. The men on the dock struggled with it, while the band stood waiting and the dignitaries milled around.

We stood at the rail, my father and I, for twenty minutes, gazing down at the gangway-lowering efforts. At 11 A.M. my father announced that he was going to go below and check the lunch menu.

"Dad," I said, suppressing the urge to add "you're crazy." "We're not eating on the ship. We're eating in Naples. It's only 11. They'll get the ramp down."

He went to check anyway. That gave me time to breathe deep and think. If he wants to eat on the ship, wants to slurp up another plate of indifferent chicken chop suey, let him. Smile and nod. Respect, respect. Yes, of course, Dad, whatever you say. Let's not go down that road again. No more Chinese food crises.

He returned. "Of course, you can have lunch on the ship," I said brightly, adding to myself, *instead of heading into frigging Napoli for a real Italian meal, you soulless fuck.*

But his interest in shipboard fare had diminished. Since we were at port, lunch was only being served in the cadet mess. The officers would not be waited upon. That took the blush off lunch on the ship. My dad didn't like having his food ladled onto his plate in front of him, he said, and certainly didn't want to carry a tray. He was as concerned about rank and station as any barrister in a Gilbert and Sullivan operetta. He claimed he had never been interested in eating on the ship, just checking proximities, being aware. He tried to jokingly pin the blame on me: I shouldn't be so uptight, so nervous. I grinned a big, insincere grin, thinking, *Yes, yes, Dad, whatever you say.*

They rigged up a temporary gangway. The band swung into "Columbia, the Gem of the Ocean" shortly after 11:30 A.M. The captain finally went ashore, where he shook hands with officials, including a guy with an ascot and a shiny suitcoat draped over his shoulders, just like someone out of a Fellini film. Two TV cameras recorded the scene.

My father pointed out a taxi bringing an officer's wife to meet the ship—hope blossomed that we wouldn't have to walk down the pier. When the taxi left, my father lifted a finger, as if to hail it, and wanly said "Hey, wait." He was agitated, talking a lot, trying to joke.

"My son is nervous," he said to an engineer we had just met. I turned wordlessly and walked away, just to get away from him. I went to another deck and hid until I noticed him, peering down a stairway, looking for me. I went over.

"No lights," he said, gesturing to the pier. "How can the cadets go ashore with no lights?"

CHAPTER 9

Spring Open the Cage

By noon we were on the pier, walking briskly toward Naples. It was indeed a long walk, over a crumbling concrete wharf strewn with broken glass, concrete blocks, and trash. We had gone maybe twenty-five yards when my father, somehow detecting an Italian police car approaching from behind, wheeled around and stuck out his thumb. The compact car stopped and we were gestured into the small back seat. We roared off. The policemen paid no attention to us during the brief trip to the head of the pier. They were relaxed, handsome, young—none of the coiled menace of Chicago cops. They seemed like two male models chatting during a lull in a photo shoot.

They dropped us off at the gate, next to a guard with a submachine gun. We got out of the car with a flurry of waves and *"grazies."* I gave my father credit: flagging down a pair of Italian cops was inspired, and not something I would have done. He still had the old moxie. It put us into the city in maximum good spirits.

Naples was beautiful, sleepy, placid. Rather than what we had expected—gangs of greasy young men, giving us hard, appraising looks, evaluating our weaknesses—the streets were filled with old gents in sports shirts and well-suited young guys jabbering into cellular phones.

It took an hour to walk to the train station. Neither of us wanted a cab. The sidewalks were crowded. It was cloudless, sunny, hot; I urged dad into a narrow place that had a candy store in the front and a bar in the back. You get that combination in Italy—bakeries and bars, ice cream parlors with bars.

The bar had a narrow green marble counter, and in my best halting Italian I ordered a beer for myself ("Beck's, *per favore*") and an orange juice for my father. Two thin soda jerks, both wearing vests and bow ties and jaunty absorbent caps, set about the task. They were charming in a brisk, crisp, 1950s fashion, like Texaco gas station attendants swarming over a Buick. Handing my father his juice, I raised my glass of beer. "Here's to Italy," I said. He walked a few feet away and stood there, awkwardly, his back to me. I remained, frozen, glass in air, the smile dying on my face, until he turned, saw me, and walked back to touch glasses. "Here's to Italy," I said again, a little coldly.

"I thought you said, 'Move away,' " my father explained.

Dad had written down the name of a restaurant near the train station from one of his guidebooks. We passed ten appealing places he wouldn't consider and finally arrived at the nondescript, family eatery whose address he had on a scrap of paper. There was a TV going inside, a blather of excited Italian, and only a few of the bare linoleum tables were occupied. The menu was in both Italian and English, the English a delight of flawed translation: "Spaghetti to the tomato"; "Cannelloni to the oven"; "Noodles to whipped cream"; "Linguine to the roses"; "Beefsteak of ster to the irons"—this meant, I realized after some thought, grilled steak. I tried to order gnocchi, got cannelloni, eventually; tried to order a glass of red wine, got—to my pleased surprise—a bottle, though it was a fizzy sort of red, Tarantello Vino da Tavola. The fizz was off-putting at first, but grew on you, and Dad was able to drink it, too. We sat there, glad to be out of sun and not walking. Despite all the time I had to prepare myself, grasping that we were in Naples drinking Italian wine was still quite a shock—as if I had stepped out of the bathroom at home and found myself in Italy, with my dad.

The train station was large, dark and modern, with all sorts of wandering-across-Europe types standing around—American kids in yak-herder caps, hikers with backpacks and walking sticks, tweedy British couples, matched as bookends, sprawling olive-skinned extended families, camped protectively around their possessions. They struck me as Romanian or Turkish, though they probably were working-class Italians.

Train tickets had been another of my father's fixations for the past month. We had parsed every detail. We must get first class. We must get reserved seats. We must get express. Without the lure of buying the tickets ahead of time, I don't think I'd have gotten my father to venture into Naples at all.

The two of us stood in a line. At the front, I leaned into the window, repeating the sentence I had memorized in Italian about buying tickets. But the train the next morning was sold out, and in trying to find another train, I slipped into English, which got me immediately dispatched to another line, for information. While I waited in that line, my father got back in the purchase line, thinking he'd be almost at the head by the time I got back. Efficiency. But the information line moved more slowly than the purchase line, and he reached the front of his line ahead of me. By the time I arrived, he had negotiated the sale of tickets himself, and I got there just in time to pay for them.

They were second-class, nonreserved, nonexpress—nothing we had discussed, ad nauseam. But they were tickets, for the 1 P.M. train to Rome the next day, and we had them, and I figured the rest would work itself out. I had visions of sharing a half-day, twenty-mile-per-hour ordeal with crates of live chickens and gypsy families, but I kept them to myself.

Mission accomplished, Dad was ready to go back to the ship, but having been denied Pompeii, I wanted to at least see the treasures that had been removed and taken to the Archeological Museum, and I talked him into getting in a cab to go with me. The cab was new and had a meter—none of the haggling that every guidebook warned about.

The museum was bold and imposing on the outside and dim and airy inside. It must have once been a palace of some sort—the main room was a gigantic ballroom, more impressive than any of the artwork on its walls. The paintings were dark, in deep browns and dull blues, with a primitive Roman air, but the mosaics were intricate and charming.

The spacious galleries, nearly empty of visitors, had French doors with bars across them, opened wide to allow cool air in from the coral-colored courtyard, and the guard in each room sat in the doorway, smoking a cigarette or reading a newspaper or just staring outside.

I went over to an unguarded window and leaned over the iron rail, gazing happily down at the ivy-covered wall opposite, trees and plants exploding above. In the distance, buildings of pink, of orange. Below in the courtyard, a scattering of ancient urns. Kids at play shouted from the next block.

Springtime in Italy. My dad joined me. "In like Flynn," I said, with a sweep of the arm.

"Careful what you lean on," he said, and walked away.

The museum also had sculpture, and I caught myself gazing closely at the draped thighs of a colossal *Aphrodite*, ten feet tall. Very lifelike. It's a bad sign when you start to fantasize about screwing a giant marble toga-clad woman holding roses. Been away from home too long, I thought, smiling at myself.

We left the museum and stood in front of it a moment before we plunged together into the city. We didn't have a goal or plan, and my father still wanted to get back to the ship. But I was drawn by the city's intrigue and beauty. Everywhere your eye settled was lovely, in a fading, decrepit way. Shuttered windows, little balconies, crumbling stucco, a sense of age and grace. I was in the cities I had built out of wooden blocks as a child—narrow streets shaded by leaping arches and walkways, curious little spindly towers, wide steps leading up to massive doors.

Nearby an immense indoor gallery—Galleria Principe di Napoli. Its entranceway looked like the Arc de Triomphe, but in rose terra-cotta with a curved glass ceiling beyond, a sweeping grid of iron. Empty, a giant, interior space with a gray marble floor and nothing in it, except for a young couple necking on a stone bench. These were the ideal urban spaces Internationalism had so screwed up. Curving plazas, grand ceremonial outdoor courtyards, colonnades topped with statues, enormous wrought-iron gates. Clock towers. The city's slumping economy had saved it from the rape of progress.

My father seemed tired. "Let's sit down," I said, directing us to a pretty outdoor cafe with tables covered in floral tablecloths and shaded by big square cotton umbrellas.

Motor scooters ground by, some carrying three people—a father, mother and child. Dad didn't say much. I read the *International Herald Tribune* and smoked a cigar. A beer, two beers.

There was a wall covered with ivy, ivy with violet flowers in it, surrounding a window.

I gazed at the windows, curtains blowing out, and felt like living here, on this street. The place was called Bar Fiorillo, and the mustachioed owner was talking to his daughter—a sturdy girl about ten, sweeping her hair back affectionately. I imagined my boys running across the cobblestones with their Italian friends, eyes afire with mischief.

We pressed on. The streets were narrow, medieval. Stores were clustered by themes, as if they had huddled together for comfort, aggregating over the centuries. A street of clothing shops, of book shops, toy stores. I stopped before a shop window adorned with old dolls. An eerie workshop, dim. There wasn't a brand or cartoon character in sight—just old china dolls, curly heads, and disembodied limbs hanging from the ceiling.

Dad kept going, I called him back. He backtracked, gave the doll shop a perfunctory glance, and continued on. His feet hurt and he wanted to accomplish his mission. With dinnertime approaching, he was looking for a fish restaurant. But when we finally did find an area with restaurants, they were closed. Italians eat late. We were used to eating on the ship just after 5 P.M., but the restaurants didn't open until 8 P.M. Now it was just six.

I spied a *gelateria*. We went inside; the ice cream looked wonderful—intense colors: deep yellows, blues, greens. We could have a sandwich first, then gelato. But Dad waved it off. His feet hurt, but he wanted fish, and the gelateria had no fish.

On the third complaint about his feet I steered us into a little church, dim and quiet inside. We sat on frail wooden chairs. The noise from the street died away. I read a blue sign on the wall: CORSI DI PREPARAZIONE AL MATRIMONIO. I didn't need my Italian class to figure that one out. It was very peaceful. Several silent old women sat ahead of us, praying.

The church had a rotunda above the altar, all columns and gold leaf and moldings run amok. I was gazing up, soaking it all in, when my father whispered. "I'm ready to go once you are." His motto. We had been there less than a minute. "Okay" I said, rising to my feet, smiling artificially, thinking, *Respect, respect.*

By 7 P.M. Dad was in a frenzy of impatience. "I don't think it's going to get us anywhere walking these streets," he said. I felt very sad, tagging after this man—my father, apparently—trying to sneak glimpses through the shop windows flying by, to soak up the street life as he strode away. He just wouldn't slow down. It was maddening.

Giving up, I asked him if he wanted to go back to the ship. He said yes and immediately stuck his arm in the air and began trying to flag a cab. I said, "Whoa, let me grab a slice of pizza—it's already past seven, dinner will be over. We'll have to eat cookies."

He followed me for a block or two, when I noticed a woman sweeping the sidewalk before an open storefront that had a menu on a stand and a few tables within. We went over. A pair of middle-aged women were fussing over a month-old baby in a pink stroller. After cooing with all the *bellas* and *bellissimos* I could muster, I asked if they would serve us dinner. They would.

The place was small, clean, rustic, painted in bright yellows and earthy reds, made even cozier by the thought that we would not have to scrounge up a bologna sandwich in the ship's kitchen. We were the only diners. The waitress brought red wine in a ceramic pitcher. My father ordered his fish. I ordered seafood fettuccini and, forgetting the warning of my Italian teacher, Mr. Dragonetti, that it just isn't done, asked for parmesan cheese. The waitress not only brought the cheese but also brought a big tablespoon, as if they were a matched set, like salt and pepper. Seeing the big spoon reminded me. I laughed, recoiling—asking for the parmesan with seafood must have tagged me as an idiot American, and the waitress figured she might as well bring the big spoon at the same time and save herself a trip. "Oh, no, no, no," I said. "*Per favore*. Not the big spoon. Please. Anything but the big spoon." I handed them both back, protesting, managing to explain that it had been a mistake. I must have conveyed my embarrassment properly because the waitress laughed, too—or maybe she was just placating the madman—and she took away the parmesan and the big spoon.

After dinner we took a cab back to the docks, but the *calliberi* would not let it on the pier. An Italian Navy facility couldn't allow just any taxicab that shows up to drive around inside. They were very sorry. We hiked twenty minutes to the ship, past debris and a pack of stray dogs, time aplenty for my father to work himself into a towering, dock-length-obsessed funk. We would never roll our luggage this way in the morning. Never! We were too important for that. A cab would be allowed on the pier. It must be allowed. This would not stand.

"I'll talk to the captain," I kept saying. Having said that, there was no need, in my mind, to think further about the matter until the captain had been spoken with. I didn't see the big deal. Worse-case scenario: we'd roll our luggage down the dock. There are grimmer fates, though not to hear my father talk about it. I trudged alongside him. The sun set and Naples began twinkling, unadmired, behind us.

Back at the ship I settled my father in our cabin and went looking for the captain. He was still ashore, but I ran into the doctor. He said he was about to enjoy one of the fine, hand-rolled cigars he bought at the factory in Barbados. Would I like one? I said yes, first ducking back into the cabin to tell my father what I was up to. Could I entice him to join us? No.

The doctor and I smoked reflectively—not on the fantail, of course, but on the walkway outside the cabin deck. He was mellow, pleased with his day exploring Naples, which sounded much better than mine, even though I felt we had had a good start. In fact, I was energized by Naples. It wasn't bad at all. I could take this, except for dad's Speedy Bunny act. I would talk to him about that. We would enjoy Italy together—which to me meant absorbing something of the flavor of the place. My dad's impatient self-containment would crack, and he'd open up to the delight of the country. I was sure of it. By week's end he'd be wearing wraparound sunglasses and his sports coat draped over his shoulders like a cape, bunching his fingertips together and tapping them excitedly in front of his face as he dickered over the price of a garish necktie at an outdoor stand. We'd slouch. We'd rent a scooter—one for the both of us. Before I was through with him we'd be strolling down the street, laughing and slapping each other on the back, pausing to unleash long wolf whistles and exaggerated puckering kisses at the pretty women rushing by.

The captain came aboard and, handing my lit cigar to the doctor, I raced up to his cabin and laid out the situation. "I'll drive you," he said, immediately. "Just let me know when you want to leave."

I conveyed this information happily back to my father, who was delighted. The captain himself! The world set right.

The next morning I delivered a speech to my father: he would have to slow down and look at things, or at least feign interest. I would not spend the next ten days tagging after him as he ran through Italy. I don't want to jog; I want to enjoy myself, at a leisurely pace. If he couldn't do that, then we would have to split up, at least for a while during the day, so I could soak in my surroundings. He could bolt through Italy alone with his eyes closed, for all I cared.

He seemed chastened, taken aback, initially. Then Dad struck on his counterargument: remember the time I read a book as we drove through the Rockies? Mom kept saying to look at the mountains, look at the mountains. But I kept my nose in the book. He was triumphant.

There is no convincing some people; whatever you tell them is just an invitation to rationalization. We had both forgotten why we were there in the first place. Having spent a month in a cabin with my dad, I was now ready to tour Italy. And my father? He was just holding on as best he could until he could get back to Colorado and kiss the ground.

We were both lying on our beds at 9 A.M., resting before our final departure from the ship. At 9:20 A.M. I swung my legs over the side of the bed. Dad leapt up, grabbed his bag, opened the door, and started dragging his suitcase out. Our train left at 1 P.M. The captain was meeting us at the foot of the gangway at 10 A.M. The train station was a fifteen-minute drive away.

"*Dad,*" I said, "let's not rush. You're rushing me." He sheepishly hauled the suitcase back. I felt like a prima donna, ordering him about. But I hated always being in a mad panic.

I left him in the room and walked the length of the ship one last time, soaking it all in. We arrive at a place before we arrive—contemplating it, imagining what it will be like, anticipating, tossing a few mental cushions ahead of us to soften the shock of the unfamiliar. And we leave before we leave, disassociating ourselves from what we have become accustomed to in order to make parting a little less difficult. Or at least I do. As I walked to the bow, running my hands over the surfaces, the ship recovered some of the strangeness it had when I first stepped aboard, a month earlier.

Dad suggested we tap a couple of cadets to carry our luggage, but I brushed that idea aside. It seemed imperial. "Boy, get our bags." So I wrestled his rolling suitcase down the stairway and ashore, then returned for mine. I stood on the pier, sweaty and winded, wondering why, left to my own devices, I take the hard way. Without Dad's prodding, I would have never asked the captain to drive us. I'd have walked, humping that bag a mile down the pier. Either the noble or the stupid route, I'm not sure. Probably a little of both.

The captain arrived and presented us with a pair of Maritime College baseball caps. My dad had expected the captain to have a driver. "I can't see him navigating those roundabouts for the first time," he said. But Ahlstrom drove us to the station in a small rented Fiat. I noticed a heavy burning smell I took to be the exhaust from the scooters. It turned out the captain had left the parking brake on. He laughed and released it. For the next week my father marveled at the captain's easygoing calm: no anger, no embarrassment, just releasing the brake with a joke about abusing rental cars. Most people, it seemed to my father and myself, waltz through life with a song. Must be nice.

* * *

The Rome train station was much larger and busier than the station in Naples. We plunged into the chaos. A monk in black robes hurried past, carrying a briefcase. A group of taxi touts tried to get their hooks into us. We ignored them, headed outside to the taxi stand, piled our luggage into a Mercedes taxi. The driver didn't know where Hotel Gregoriana or the Via Gregoriana was, and just as navigation seemed about to break down my father leaned forward and said "Spanish Steps" and off we went.

Rome flashed by: big, bright, summery. It had none of the tumbledown seedy charm of Naples, and, in the cab, I regretted fleeing Naples so quickly. Rome seemed sterile. We had left Greenwich Village for Park Avenue.

Walking through the neighborhood around our hotel, I began to appreciate Rome. I loved that the sewer covers were emblazoned with "S.P.Q.R."—an abbreviation of *Senatus Populusque Romanus,* or "The Roman Senate and People"—the same initials Centurions carried at the top of tall staffs as their legions marched into battle. A civic tradition dating back two thousand years. In Chicago, we think Daley is steeped in tradition because his dad was mayor way back in the 1950s.

I told Dad that Naples had struck me as beautiful. He said that going there was always seen as a requirement for living a full life. That's what "Go to Naples and die" meant—you can't die until you've seen it. Now he tells me.

Next morning we were up before 5 A.M., and by 6 were working away—me, sitting cross-legged, typing up notes, a map spread on the bed, my father, in his blue-striped summer pajamas, writing postcards. A pleasant breeze came in from the open windows, carrying noises from the street, trucks grinding past, doors opening, voices.

"How do you spell Rebecca?" my father asked.

"R-E-B-E-C-C-A," I said. Rebecca is my sister's youngest daughter.

"Do you think she'd mind if I called her 'Becky'?" he said.

I told him I've never heard her mom call her that.

"We'll respect her mother's wishes, then," he said. A long silence, both of us, writing.

"This is one of the most moving experiences of the trip," my father said. "I'm writing a postcard to my granddaughters and signing it 'Love grandpa.' "

I smiled. "You must have sent them postcards before."

"On what basis?" he asked.

"Well, you traveled places."

"We *called*," he said. "That's why I made up my mind I wanted to send something to the grandkids. I didn't want to just ignore them. I mean, it sounds like a trivial thing to do. Of course, I'm not sending cards to your kids. They're too young."

"To realize they got a postcard from their grandpa?" I asked. He laughed, held up his hands, and said, "Say no more. I'll do it."

He seemed very happy.

"What a pleasure to address it: 'Miss Rina Steinberg' "—he said, referring to my brother's daughter. "I'm going to spell it the way she wants to spell it. . . ."

"And not the way Mom wants to spell it?" I said. "I think that's a good idea."

My brother named his daughter Rina, but pronounces it "Lena," the way Japanese would pronounce an "R." This was a mystery to all of us, particularly since his son's name is Ryan but not pronounced "Lion." No matter how many times I asked Sam, I never understood the reasoning. Eventually I gave up trying to figure it out, something my parents never could do.

Dad kept writing. "Arlington Heights . . . *Illinois?*" he asked.

"Yes, Dad, Illinois," I said. "You know that."

"To me, it's new," he said. A long pause. "*Grandpa* doesn't have an *h* on the end, does it?"

I let the question dangle for a moment at arm's length, admiring it like a Christmas ornament. A month together had not blunted my father's endless ability to amaze me. "No, Dad," I said, eventually. "No *h* on the end."

He stared at the postcard. "You sure?"

"Yes, I'm sure."

"Because it looks strange," he said.

"I'm positive. G-R-A-N-D-P-A. No *H*. You can't mean you've never written it before."

"I don't think so."

"You have a granddaughter ten years old."

"My granddaughters won't speak to me on the phone," he said. "I have tried a number of times. They won't speak to Mom."

I didn't know that. "That's terrible," I said. "Debbie should make them."

"She doesn't."

"Why?"

"Because she's a basket case," he said. "Look, I don't know. It's all terribly sad. What can you say?"

Not much. My older sister was the great tragedy of our family. As a teenager she had been pretty and smart; she loved Eugene O'Neill and Shakespeare and Laurence Olivier. We sat together on the couch, watching TV, laughing at the stage-chewing evil of his *Richard III*. Moving into her bedroom after she went to Ohio State changed my life because I started reading the books on her shelves—*Death of a Salesman* and *Long Day's Journey into Night*. But something awful happened to her—nobody seems to have figured out what, herself included—and she ended up one of those broken people, medicated and sagging under the weight of her problems. She married a sallow mope, moved to Dallas, had a couple of daughters, tried to hold together a normal life, but everything fell apart. Years of hospitals, of medications. There really wasn't anything to be done anymore. We had tried to help, early on, flying down to Dallas as a family to play our role in her counseling sessions, then sending money and keeping close tabs on the latest progress or setback. But as the battle turned into a war and then a long, endless siege, my father, brother, and I had drifted off, emotionally, content that she was out of the hospital and living on her own, sort of, while my mother clung on, as though if she pretended everything was all right long enough, someday it might be. I was hardened by the fact that Debbie had never been a particularly nice older sister—in fact, she had been selfish and mean, and I viewed her madness as a natural extension of who she had been before. I hadn't seen Debbie in five years—she had never met my children or, worse in my eyes, expressed an interest in meeting them. That really put a shine on my armor. I made a point to phone her on her birthday to exchange pleasantries and silently confirm that nothing had changed, then let the line go dead for another six months or a year.

To get away from the subject, we started talking about the day before, at the central post office. I had gone to deposit a letter into one of the red suitcase-sized metal mailboxes used in Italy. It was stuffed so full that the three letters I put in wouldn't go down. This was at the central post office in Rome. Imagine the hinterlands; the mail must be compressed like dried tea. After the third letter, I decided to pull them all back out and put my letters in a less-filled box, my irrational concern being, I suppose, that someone would come along and pluck out my mail.

Dad had been horrified.

"There were *carabinieri* at the door," my father said. "I said to myself, *'There must be an embassy in Rome.'*" He had envisioned my going to an Italian prison for pilfering the mails.

Breakfast was brought up on a tray: a big pitcher of hot coffee, a smaller pitcher of milk, fresh rolls and croissants and biscuits, cheese and jam. Joy. The room had a TV, and we watched news of Kosovo. After a month without TV, it seemed a fascinating appliance.

We took a cab to the Vatican Museum, just opening for the day. My father had balked at going, when I first brought up the idea in Naples. "I've seen the Vatican," he said.

"When?" I asked.

"1954," he answered. I told him it was time to go back. He had resisted, but I worked on him, using the threat of insisting upon Pompeii as a lever. Eventually he agreed.

Remembering the small church in Naples, I checked my watch as we went into the Sistene Chapel—10:32 A.M.—just in case my father tried to shoo us out after five minutes. I was coiled like a spring, waiting. But he didn't. We snaked through the jostling herd of tourists, tipping our heads back so far to look up that I worried about toppling backward.

Everyone has seen images of Michelangelo's work—God's finger about to touch Adam's, the various saints. But a lifetime of previews didn't prepare me for the scale. So enormous. So high up. The effect on the crowd was not what you'd expect from people viewing a famous 400-year-old artwork, but rather the sort of electric excitement you'd expect from onlookers at an unfolding dramatic event. It was as if we were watching a volcano erupt. We stayed a long time.

My father and I went inside St. Peter's, into the vast darkness beyond the portal, passing the guards stopping immodestly dressed women.

I should probably just say that the place defies description and leave it at that. St. Peter's Basilica is an eloquent dissertation in stone on the limits of language or technology to reproduce experience. Nothing I read about it, no photograph or film, in any way prepared me for the mind-warping grandeur, the incredible dream vista of interior space. My father and I spoke while we were there—I remember the sound of our voices disappearing, echoless, into the still air. But I have no idea what we said—it was just a background buzz. I was stunned. Words failed me. *Thought* almost failed me, and I fell into inarticulate wonder. It was the most fantastic thing I had ever seen in my life.

What really struck me was the chutzpa, if that is the proper word under the circumstances, of the place. Barely out of the ignorant stink of the Dark Ages, they licked their thumbs and held them out at arm's length, squinting, sighting the horizon, and said, "Okay, let's build the place like *this*. We'll have the roof two hundred, no, make that *three hundred* feet high. . . ."

My father and I had dinner near our hotel, at a restaurant called Ostera. It was Kent's second birthday and my parents' wedding anniversary, though my father didn't realize the former and I didn't realize the latter.

We toasted both occasions.

After dinner we lingered at the top of the Spanish Steps, soaking in the night scene: kids sitting on the steps, talking in the darkness, and artists selling their work. Walking back down the dark street toward our hotel, Dad asked, out of the blue, whether I had felt happy and secure growing up.

For some reason, perhaps being tired at the end of the day, discretion failed me, and I answered with reflexive honesty. "Of course not" I said, matter-of-factly. "You were moody and unpredictable. You were always off somewhere. For a while I thought you were going to leave Mom, and I was looking forward to that. Then it never happened."

This staggered him, but I didn't feel any malice—sort of a calm buffer of detachment.

He began his counterargument, but I cut him off with: "I'm sorry, I thought you asked me how I felt. Never mind." He began arguing again. I repeated my line, and it finally sunk in.

Back at the room, we talked about a lot of things—we seemed to be in a rancor-free zone after our incredible day in Rome. I told him about the Cleveland Indians game that Grandpa Irving, my mother's father, had taken me to when I was four or five. His report that I had more interest in eating hot dogs than in watching the game became the kiss-off pretext by which I was never taken to another baseball game ever again. My father and I had never gone together, not once, despite my love for baseball, despite living forty-five minutes from Cleveland Municipal Stadium. The next game I went to was when I was thirteen—old enough to be dropped off by myself. It wasn't right. He should have roused himself to go, at least once. It would have meant something to me, then and now. And even if he didn't want to go—which he obviously didn't—it was wrong to put the blame on me, as if he would have taken a less hungry son.

I told him how the previous summer I took Ross, then two, to his first game at Wrigley Field. I was eager to take him, and would have gone sooner but two seemed about as early as I could hope he would get anything from the experience. He wore my old Indians cap and what he charmingly called my "baseball mitten." The game lasted nearly four hours, and Ross sat through every minute of it. And—not that it mattered—he declined a hot dog.

That evening I had excitedly described the big game to my mother over the telephone. Her only reaction was to bring up the old hot dog libel. She thought it was funny. I icily told her that the statute of limitation on a fat boy eating too many hot dogs at a baseball game is thirty years, and she should let it go.

This story seemed to affect my dad. He had been distracted, he said. His career. He wished he had paid more attention. And was I that dissimilar, he wanted to know. He saw me in action on the ship.

"You work too hard—all that effort poured into the class," he said. "Why? You should have just told them you realized you didn't want to do it."

I told him that I *did* want to do it. I had made a commitment. I had a responsibility. I wanted the kids to learn. And I always work hard, I said. I see this period as the time of my life to produce, to make hay while the sun shines, and since I don't neglect my family, this trip notwithstanding, I don't feel bad about it.

We sat on our respective beds in the dark room, staring straight ahead, the only light filtering in from the streets. He said, again, that his big regret in life was not spending more time with his kids when they were growing up. I told him he was repeating that mistake now with his grandkids. "You just aren't interested," I said.

He had no reply. I knew that the zing of his Colorado mountain lifestyle was more attractive to him than anything my brother or myself or our kids had to offer, and there was nothing more to say about it. You can't change people. You can make them *do* things, but you can't make them *want* things. I had tried and it didn't work. I could press my father into going to a baseball game with me, now that I was an adult, if I wanted to. But why, if he wasn't interested? I might as well kidnap him. It was too late, anyway. At least I had gotten him on the ship; at least he had consented to spend a week and a half in Italy with me. That had to be enough. Anything else was asking too much. I couldn't expect him to *like* it. I couldn't expect the scales to fall from his eyes. Besides, we didn't need epiphanies—he wasn't going to slap himself on the forehead and announce that he was moving to Chicago to teach his grandsons how to whittle. It was pointless and counter-productive for me to keep trying to get him to change, just as it was harmful for my mother to keep expecting Debbie to somehow become Grace Kelly, if only mailed a sufficient number of little helpful lifestyle clippings from the newspaper.

The hour grew late. My father and I both agreed that nobody changes. All you can hope is to understand, and sometimes you can't even do that. We called it a day.

Heading downstairs the next morning, my father said he had something he wanted to ask the hotel owner. The train to Florence, of course. What was the best way to get tickets? The owner suggested the

American Express office. I wanted to get to the Colosseum when it opened at 9 A.M., but agreed to a detour, to the AmEx office at the base of the Spanish Steps. I figured the only way to keep my father from spending the next twenty-four hours obsessing over the tickets was to buy them now. Respect, respect.

We filled out paperwork, and were kept cooling our heels at AmEx for twenty minutes, then told that the computers were down. This was the Italy I had expected. I finally convinced Dad that we could come back later and we left, having blown a half hour.

The Colosseum was a big pile of bricks baking in the sun. Then to the synagogue, of course. It was not centuries old—synagogues hadn't been permitted until the nineteenth century. Still, it was attractive, grand, gleaming white outside, where policemen patrolled with machine guns. To get in we had to pass through narrow electric security doors that took a sharp 90-degree turn. No church needed that.

Inside, the synagogue was Babylonian deco, and the tour guide, apologizing for the security, explained that in 1982 the Black September terrorist group had burst in, shot up the place, and killed a child. We couldn't take pictures, lest terrorists posing as tourists use photos to plan another attack.

After, we walked along the Tiber. Dad's mind zeroed in on the train schedule. I tried to deflect him.

"Since we know there's a train at 10:55, why don't we just go to the station, get our tickets, and get on?" I said.

"Fine," Dad said. "We'll do whatever you like." We walked in silence. The Tiber rolled by. "What if the train is full?" he said.

I pointed out that the tickets we bought for Rome had no time on them, no particular train. They were just generic tickets. "How did our getting tickets to Rome guarantee that the train wouldn't be full?" I asked. To me it was very clear. But that wasn't what annoyed me. I was frustrated by my father's simultaneous insistence that he would do what I wanted—his show of flexibility—and his urging we should go back to AmEx and get the tickets. We could do whatever I liked so long as it was what he wanted to do.

The trip to Florence took ninety minutes. In the worst case, the nightmare scenario, we could stand in the bar car and drink two beers and we'd be there. We didn't even need tickets. We could buy them on the train.

I gave up. We went back to AmEx for another half hour, and found the same commotion we had left that morning. My father yelled at the woman who had waited on us earlier that day. We had filled out a form for the tickets, but then the computers went down. "Why haven't our tickets been saved?" he wanted to know. Then they announced that their computers crashed again—maybe they do that once an hour to clear the room.

Back at the hotel he kept up the charade. He didn't care if we bought tickets ahead of time. "Fine, let's go have dinner then," I would say, and he would stare straight ahead, motionless. It approached six o'clock. The travel agents would be closing. At about a quarter to six I said, "Oh, the hell with it," and we went out. The first travel agent was closed. The second didn't sell train tickets. The third did—unreserved tickets that could be used on any train to Florence. The agent said they couldn't sell any other kind.

The next morning, we had a few minutes before we needed to go to the station, so took a stroll back to the Spanish Steps. My father was pointing out sights—a door, the color of a building, a Spanish cross. This was so unlike him that I almost thought he was mocking me, extracting some kind of subtle revenge for my demanding that he notice things.

An hour and forty-five minutes to Florence, through rolling farm country. As old as Italy is, it still has lots of farmland, just like the United States, only with cypress trees that look like topiary.

If I had been apprehensive rolling into Rome, arriving at Florence was a thrill. Medieval yet clean, as if they had disassembled the city, washed the stones, then put them back together. Our hotel, the Hotel Pendini, was on the Piazza della Repubblica, a giant square. It was a building you'd never see in America—jumping across the street, with a long colonnade filled with newsstands and T-shirt vendors.

We dropped our bags and headed for lunch. Dad asked the clerk for recommendations, and he sent us to Paola, which had been in the same spot for 150 years—or roughly since Chicago was a fur-trading town on the far periphery of the newborn American Republic.

We ate our best meal in Italy there. The waiter, who wore a crisp white jacket, spoke English with that perfect half-polite, half-brusque waiter demeanor. He brought a crate of dirt-encrusted mushrooms over to show us how fresh they were. My father and I drank wine and talked about music; I had been watching music videos at the hotel in Rome.

My father said he had never been to a pop music concert of any kind in his life. Never went to hear a singer. I asked him why, as stunned as if he had said he never tasted chocolate.

He said he never felt inclined.

I felt enormous sympathy for my father. Music cast him so clearly as a person deprived. I had so many good music memories, so many songs that seemed to reach right into my brain and give my hypothalamus a big squeeze.

I knew my father liked some music. He liked *Carmen*, liked *Bolero*. But it still seemed a faint appreciation, a blind man running his fingers over the textured surface of a painting. In Barbados, we had been walking through the coral-colored mall when we passed a music store. A tape machine on a chair by the door was playing Bruce Springsteen's "Streets of Philadelphia." I stopped. "I love this song," I told my father. "It's so sad. Listen." He listened for one second, head cocked, as if straining to hear a pinging noise that somebody thought was coming from a car engine. Then he just walked away, as if hearing nothing, without comment, leaving me standing by the tape machine.

We walked a little after lunch, but he felt tired, so I whisked him back to the hotel and dropped him off to take a nap about 3 P.M. It was a liberating feeling, to clatter down the wide slate steps of the hotel, alone, and out into Florence.

The Piazza della Repubblica led into a tony shopping area—lots of purses and women's fashions. I stumbled around, soaking everything in, until I turned a corner and there, suddenly, was the Duomo—the Cathedral of Santa Maria del Fiore. An enormous church of multi-hued marble—greens and whites and soft reds. I walked all around it, impressed. I had had no suspicion that it would be there; had not, I realized then, read up on Florence or given myself any idea of what I would be seeing. My father is so set on examining every aspect of what's ahead that I overcompensate and go in blind. I did know there was an Uffizi Gallery, only because the mafia had made headlines by exploding a bomb there a few years earlier. But that was it.

Dad was just waking up when I got back to the hotel, so I went to the comfortable, shabby-elegant lobby and had a drink at a small gray marble table. When Dad was ready, I told him I had a surprise. We re-traced my route that had led to my rounding a corner and encountering the Duomo. I told him to close his eyes and walked him, holding his arm, the last dozen steps.

"Okay, now open them," I said. The Duomo.

He was impressed. We had finally reached an even keel. For a few hours.

After dinner I called home. Ross picked up. "Are you coming home soon?" he said. "Do you miss me? Is your heart broken?"

Then Edie got on. She was very upset. All sorts of troubles with the boys misbehaving. She began to cry. The woman we had hired to help her with the boys while I was gone had abruptly quit, fed up. They had thrown things at her.

"Hang in there," I said. My mind was racing. I tried to comfort her. A few more days, I implored, I'll be home soon. Then everything would be all right. Hold on.

"Do you remember me?" I asked.

"Not really." She sniffed.

We couldn't talk that much. She kept being interrupted by the boys, who were hitting each other with toy fishing poles. "You're hitting people!" she yelled at them. Eventually things calmed down. Edie brightened, and told me she had taken the boys out for Kent's birthday, and the waiters had grouped around and sang "Happy Birthday." Afterward Ross, wide-eyed, had asked "Mommy, how did they *know* it was Kentie's birthday?"

The call upset me. I was larking through Italy with my dad while my wife was struggling. The cracking strain and pressure behind her voice when she had shouted "You're hitting people!" Like a piece of lumber snapping. I told my father I was going to Murphy's—a little Irish bar situated, improbably, in the shadow of the Duomo. He said he'd go with me; he was worried about me and wanted to keep me company. I appreciated the gesture even as I resented his presence. I could have used the time alone.

My father sat outside at one of the little tables, and I went inside to get his beer and my whiskey. We struck up a conversation with a sloe-eyed, tousle-haired young man who said he was from Manchester but kept sliding into a vaguely Euro-trash accent. He said, variously, that he was a law student and an architect and an actor. I figured he was a young person pretending, badly, and told him so. Probably a German. I must have been right because he expressed only mild irritation. Had he really been from Manchester, he would have killed me.

* * *

The next morning I woke up hung over and worried about Edie. As I was brushing my teeth, Dad reached in the bathroom, trying to put on another light for me, and instead shut the bathroom light off, momentarily. I flashed him an annoyed look and he called me on it. I denied it, but he was right. I was tired, mad. Maybe a day in Florence will fix me, I thought.

It didn't. We left our umbrellas in the room, despite threatening skies, and walked to the Accademia. Michelangelo's *David* left me cold. I had seen it too many times already. I don't think I would have looked at it twice if it were in some long line of statues—another naked man with a disproportionately big head and big hands. The rest of the museum was unmoving, except for the *Slaughter of the Innocents.* We had to linger because outside was a downpour.

The rain subsided, somewhat, and we made a run for it. Dad bolted for the hotel. I hurried after, dodging ladies with umbrellas, darting across streets. Every time I paused under an awning or in a doorway, he got farther and farther away. Last I saw of him, he was fifty yards beyond me, a pink Madras shirt zipping across the *piazza* on a gloomy wet day.

I slowed down, sad, letting the rain pelt me. I thought of earlier in the spring—getting caught by another rainstorm, this time as Edie and I strolled the boys home from the playground in Lincoln Park. We had run, laughing together, me leaning forward and grasping the handle of the stroller—a long double stroller I referred to as "the bus"— practically at nose level, as the rainstorm soaked us. When we couldn't get any wetter, we both stopped, though almost at the apartment, and turned our smiling faces up to receive the warm rain, giddy. It was fun, sticking together. I can't imagine leaving Ross and Kent behind to run for cover myself after they become adults any more readily than I could contemplate leaving them in their stroller in the park while I took off for home. The abandonment would be less criminal in the first case, but it would be abandonment all the same.

My father and I changed clothes, dried off, rested. I didn't say anything about our race back to the hotel. Then, with the weather clearing, we headed to the Uffizi Gallery. There was a long line. Dad suggested that we could probably go to the front and slip the guard some money. "This is Italy," he said.

"What else do we have to do?" I said, testily. I didn't want to be a pushy American. We weren't the suave types who palm guards money and slip ahead of lines. We were the sort who get into screaming arguments with offended museum officials and end up in jail.

I contemplated cutting the trip short—just by a day. Leave Florence tomorrow, spend a day in Venice, then go home a day early, on Tuesday. I was starting to lose it. Wednesday seemed so far away. Another full day in Florence. We had seen everything. What could be left?

But I'd never know how that extra day could affect things. The obvious dramatic highpoint hadn't happened. I hated the idea of cutting the trip short—even by a day. It would hang over my head forever. Damn everything, I thought. Don't back out now, with the end in sight. Don't quit when the going gets rough. Remember Oliver Hazard Perry. Don't give up the ship.

We mailed postcards. I sent Edie a detail of Botticelli's *Venus* with the note, "I saw this and I thought of you." We headed back to AmEx—never too early to worry about our train tickets to Venice. Dad was insistent this time—no more "it's up to you" charade. They were closed for lunch.

So instead, off to the temple, our fourth of the trip—Charleston, Bridgetown, Rome, and now Florence. The neighborhoods became plainer, dingier. Six blocks away from the Piazza della Repubblicca it seemed a completely different city, of auto repair shops and vacant buildings. We got where the synagogue was supposed to be, but couldn't find it, even after asking a few locals.

Dad and I exchanged harsh words. I had gone up to ask somebody where the temple was, pointing to the location on a map with my finger. My father stepped up behind me and pointed too, his finger beside mine. His echoing of whatever I said, as if I were an idiot who couldn't make himself understood, had already been bugging me, and I brushed his finger away from mine. He chewed me out, obscenely. When we finally found the place, it was closed. On the way back, I thought it had to be a chemical thing. Maybe I'm sick. Just yesterday I was delighted to be here, in love with Florence. Now I felt horrible and wanted to go home.

Before dinner I went to the hotel's little lobby bar and got a Scotch, poured from a dusty bottle of Four Roses. I wasn't going to—I figured a day off would be salutary—but I felt so crappy, physically, I thought a drink would be a good idea. And it was. The whiskey, two of them, put me in a better frame of mind. Dad joined me at the little marble table in the lobby, and my mood elevated.

Sunday was Father's Day. Edie had packed a small present—a tiny *Star Wars* book, picked for its size and later utility with the boys. I wished Dad a happy Father's Day, and he, slightly surprised, returned the sentiment. We shook hands.

My father is not a big believer in holidays. I don't, for instance, think he ever gave me a birthday present of any kind, at least not one that I remember. That sounds like a resentful sentiment, but it isn't. I never expected one from him. He could be very generous—on foreign trips or when a particular item struck his fancy. He became fascinated, for instance, with the German building set, Fischer Technik, and cleaned out the Cleveland department stores of it, stripped their shelves, buying armfuls of boxes. It was a delightful piece of engineering—cams and differentials and worm-gear motors, its basic gray building blocks machined so precisely they made Lego blocks look like they were baked from clay. You could not only construct cranes and treaded tanks with Fischer Technik but also working stoplights. While the suspicion nagged that he was really buying the sets for himself, we kids certainly benefited, and I was proud of the zealous, money-be-damned way he amassed the stuff.

We decided to return to the synagogue. Outside, a military band was playing under the gallery of the hotel—some sort of race was going on. I wanted to stay and soak in the scene, but Dad insisted on pushing forward. We had a mission: there was a tour to get to. He would not stand, not pause, to listen to the band, but just blew by. I lingered for a moment, then, mad, set after him across the plaza, umbrella up against a light rain.

We signed up for the tour. Outside, the building was Moorish, mosquelike, complete with minarets and a soaring dome arabesqued in red, orange, and blue. The pews were delicate, wooden, almost like colonial writing desks, with little locked compartments for prayer books and religious materials. The congregation proclaimed their names on metal plaques: Alfiero Borghini, U. Sciunnach, Vittorio Scitrug. The Germans had used the synagogue as a stable during the war, then tried to blow it up when they pulled out of Italy. But the building had withstood their attempts to mine it.

The sun was out when we left the synagogue, and I was boosted by its beauty and plucky survival in the face of the Nazis.

The fortieth day of our trip dawned. The same span of time Noah was on the ark. I had stopped trying to make sense out of our odyssey. Now I was just trying to get through it. I would figure out later what it meant, I told myself.

Morning came slowly. People singing in the square had kept me up at night. I felt better after a shower, but Dad was grim. Departure day and still no tickets. "I'm going to breakfast," he announced at 8 A.M., opening the door to leave. That startled me.

"Don't you want me to go with you?" I said. Forty days together and we still didn't mesh, still weren't at ease around each other. I felt a chill of premonition. What are the odds we'll get through the next two days without problems? Slim.

At a quarter to nine Dad said we should go to the American Express office, a five-minute walk away, to buy our train tickets to Venice. I sighed and went. We got there ten minutes early. A scattering of people out front. "Let's walk around the block; no point in just staring at the building," I said. We strolled around the block, past the structure that Florence fobs off as Dante's home. I had gone through it the day before, by myself, trying to pay tribute to the man who wrote *The Inferno*—"Midway through my life's journey, I found myself lost in a dark wood"—by visiting what turned out to be a sham constructed by the city to suck in tourists. Fitting, somehow.

We returned just as AmEx was opening the doors. People poured in and bolted for the windows. Only one couple was in front of us at the train ticket window. But they were enough. It took them almost a half hour to get their tickets. We cooled our heels.

The 12:40 P.M. train was booked solid—a triumph for my father—so we got tickets on the 2:40 P.M. The clerk said they were the last two reserved seats available and they were in the smoking section to boot. "Good thing we didn't wait to go to the station," my father said, pointedly. I let him have his victory. No sense in arguing now. Still, the process took a while, and I suggested, several times, that he go sit down, or wait outside, or something. I didn't quite say, "Get away from me," but I might as well have because nothing worked. He wouldn't hear of going anywhere. He was staying put, supervising my purchase of the tickets, making sure I didn't try to sneak Second Class on him. This time we were going to get it right. He would see to it. We stood silently, together, waiting. His presence couldn't have annoyed me more if he had settled the point of his chin on my shoulder and let his weight bear down. Finally, I was issued a receipt and directed to a second window, where a pair of young women were talking to the clerk. Some sort of problem being resolved over the telephone—one of the women had an expired credit card, apparently. The clerk, on hold, gestured me to hand her my receipt. I did so, sliding it across the counter, and she began the paperwork. I waited, staring into space, rocking on my heels, my father hovering beside.

Then it exploded—in the span of five seconds. A clerk opened the window next to ours and my dad stepped smartly over to it. The clerk asked for his receipt, and Dad turned to look at me. "What should I do, take it back from her?" I said, in a peeved tone, gesturing toward the teller who had my paperwork.

Dad got very mad. "I don't have to put up with this shit," he said. "Fuck you."

"You think this . . ." I began, then the anger overwhelmed me and I bolted out of the office, pushing my way past two startled guys behind me. I stood in the Via Dante Alighieri, trembling.

Pedestrians flowed around me, oblivious. I stood there, fuming but uncertain what to do. Unable to think of something better, I walked back into the AmEx office, where Dad was just getting my receipt from the clerk. I signed it, hands shaking, then brought it back to the original window to get the tickets.

Tickets in hand, I walked out into the street. He followed, and I turned on him. What was that for? I demanded, poking him hard with my index finger. What the *fuck* was wrong with him? I poked him again and he batted my finger away.

"Don't you dare touch me," he said, forcefully. "I'm still your father. You touch me again and I'll belt you in the jaw. You can't treat me like this."

"Treat you like this? Treat you like what? What did I do?" I shrieked, aghast, pedestrians tossing us glances as they picked up speed passing us. "A sour expression? You're the one who cursed me out. I had a sour expression because I hate you hovering over me all the time. Hate it. You've been doing it the whole trip. Jesus. That's always been your problem. You can't goddamn step back and let somebody *do* something. God, I'm sorry we took this trip. What a disaster. A waste. A gut-wrenching nightmare from hell, to be with you."

"And you think you're a joy to be around?" my father said. "I've got news for you, mister."

We glared at each other.

"Let's meet at the hotel at 1 P.M.—you're not fit company to be with," I said.

"I don't need to go to Venice," he said, suddenly calm. "I could just go to the airport and go home. I don't need this."

"That's fine," I said, bitterly, striding away. "Good idea. Go ahead. Go home. Good-bye."

He turned and walked away. I went back into the AmEx office—I needed to cash some travelers' checks—then spun around, and immediately left, running after him, catching up a block away.

"I don't know why you're being this way," he said. "You're always overreacting. Always too sensitive, getting worked up. You're the only person who thinks this way about me. Nobody else has this problem. Everyone else thinks I'm just fine."

"Everyone else thinks you're a *prick*!" I shouted, losing all control now. "Sam thinks you're a prick. Mom thinks you're a prick. Debbie thinks you're a prick. I think you're a prick. And you know why? You're a prick! You've always been a prick. You'll always be a prick."

We chewed at each other for a few more minutes, but eventually our tempers cooled. We wandered, miserably, me tagging a few steps behind him. This was stupid, I thought, a stupid end to a stupid trip taken by two stupid people. That could be the title: *Two Stupid People Having a Bad Time at Sea,* by Neil Steinberg.

"This is stupid," I said, and I extended my hand and he shook it, but we did not brighten or make conversation. We walked over the Ponte Vecchio. Shopping—he was looking for something for Mom, finally buying a scarf. We went to the room to finish packing.

At eleven, I got up, walked over to the Duomo to see it one more time. I was mad at myself for getting angry, but it also seemed somehow inevitable. Quite the capstone. My moment of obvious high drama at last. I go on a trip to get closer to my father and end up disliking him even more than I did before we left, if that was possible. All those pop psychology books were a load of hooey. The assumption we always make, in our optimistic American way, is that difficulties are merely based on misunderstanding, on miscommunication. Talk it out, reach, grow, understand, and all will be well. Which is a big honking lie because sometimes the problem is that you understand all too well, and would welcome a bit of confusion. My father was a selfish person, obsessed with his personal comfort and gazing at his little mobile of borrowed ideas as it wheeled around in the breeze. He had sprung from selfish people, and passed that selfishness on to me like a hereditary illness. I was cursed, doomed to crushing, hyper self-awareness, staring at a spot on my shoe, missing it all. Missing my life.

It was deeply sad to walk all the way around the Duomo, this gigantic piece of gorgeous human vision, this straining grasp toward grace and God, while trying to sort out a petty spat with my dad. It made me feel crappy and small, or should I say, crappier and smaller.

Lack of love—that was obvious. Not enough in my heart and less in his. Neither of us had learned anything. I was mad at myself for letting it happen, but it happened so fast, like a coiled spring. One second I was standing in line at the AmEx, my mind blank, waiting. The next I was in the street, screeching like a beast. The trip was shot to hell in ten seconds. Whose fault? Mine, for the snide comment? My father's, for butting in, for insisting on taking charge? Both of ours, for being idiots? A trap I couldn't see my way out of.

The street filled with strangers. Italians. Tourists. Such a big world. So few people you love, and those you do love, half the time you can hardly get along with. Was it worth even trying? I thought again about ending it early. Forget Venice. Get home to my real family. But we were so close. Venice was the one place I had really wanted to see, ever since I read Thomas Mann's *Death in Venice* as a teenager. I couldn't imagine spending the rest of my life saying, "Yeah, I got within spitting distance of Venice, but gave up and skeedaddled home because my father was driving me crazy." Anything but that.

I returned to the room and made him give me a hug, which he did, stiffly. "Mom isn't here to make us make up," I said. He didn't say anything. I checked out of the hotel—ka-*floosh*, another $500 down the toilet. With the anger no longer coursing through my veins, the fight looked particularly petty and small and meaningless. An expression, a few words, sparking the explosive gas of deep visceral dislike that this trip had blown into us. But why blame the trip? We didn't like each other at all. We never liked each other. I hadn't liked him since I was ten years old. He just happened to be my dad. Lots of people have nothing to do with their fathers. I could be one of them. Easily.

About 1 P.M. he said we should get to the train station. Called for a cab. It was downstairs in less than a minute. We arrived at the train station an hour and a half early.

My father found a luggage cart and consolidated our luggage. I sat and put my head down on my arms on the cart. "How are you feeling?" he asked.

"Not too good," I said. "My face feels hot, and I'm still upset about this morning."

"That's past," he said, rubbing my back, which made it indeed past, and I felt better.

Twenty minutes before the train was due, we moved in front of the schedule board, in a central part of the station, so as to be positioned to rush to the train platform when it was announced. Even though we had our first-class, reserved seats—finally—Dad still wanted to bolt onto the platform the moment we knew where the train would arrive.

I never figured out where my father's anxiety about trains came from. I'm sure some Freudian could venture a guess, but I won't.

You'd think, by the way he acted, that if you miss a train, the conductors march you out behind the station and shoot you. I've missed planes before. You get on the next one. It isn't that big a deal.

The train arrived and we boarded, but not before a comic bolt to the end of the platform. I told him that the first-class section would be behind the engine, closest to the station. It only made sense. But still seeking data, he asked a passing American college student if she knew where first class would be when the train arrived, and she said at the far end. So while the train was pulling in, he was racing toward the end of the platform, with me following like a pull-toy duck, dragging our luggage cart. At least I was able to smile at it, privately, and not concentrate on the fact that he had so easily abandoned my opinion in favor of a passing stranger's. We got to the end, then backtracked, car by car. It was a long train, and we were sweaty and winded by the time we climbed aboard the proper car, right behind the engine.

We sat separately—in our particular reserved seats—while those with unreserved seats sat together and partially filled in the empty space around us. Despite what the AmEx guy had told me—that these were the last two seats left—the train was two-thirds empty. I realized there were a limited number of reserved seats—for the rare control freaks such as ourselves. The rest were unreserved. We could have gotten on the train that morning. But I didn't care. It was all a blessing. At least I didn't have to sit next to my father. No one sat near me. I had a group of four seats to myself and felt, almost for the first time in Italy, the pure thrill of traveling somewhere. I pulled out my computer and worked on columns. I went forward to check on him once, but he was chatting away with some woman, happy. He never noticed me, and I decided to just enjoy being without his company for a while. The mountainous Tuscan countryside slid by. The seats were red with black lines forming biscotti-like shapes. A little gray table folded out.

Safe on the train, I was able to reflect on the fight that morning. All that anger: so unattractive. I knew what I was upset about—having this guy looking over my shoulder—but what was bothering him? Lack of respect? I was there at the AmEx, where I didn't want to be, buying the reserved tickets I knew we didn't need. Wasn't that enough? The train was mostly empty, but they reserved us in separate parts. Italy. Once again, he put all his intense faith in a system that didn't work, and none at all in me.

My father, raised in the 1930s and 1940s, believed in systems, believed in authority. And I, raised in the 1960s and 1970s, believed in self-reliance, in skepticism. For him growing up, trust in authority led the nation out of the Depression and won the war. For me, trust in authority got you killed in Vietnam. Perhaps those two opposites will never attract.

Or maybe it came from having his father waiting at home, hiding behind the newspaper, ready to pounce on any fault, to ridicule any weakness. At least I had better than that. My father might have ignored me, but he never mocked me. Give him credit for that.

I should have kept my cool at the AmEx office. Can't let things deteriorate again. Venice was our last, final chance to end on an up note. Two days. I could do it. I would do it.

CHAPTER 10

Solace to the Downcast Heart

Venice announced itself with a long causeway, the water high and green and wintry on both sides of the tracks. A drizzling rain.

My father and I stepped out of the train and were in Venice. We rolled our suitcases out of the station and to the *vaporetto* stop, marked by big barber poles. We got on the right boat, which peeled off into the canal. One palace after another. Thin, arched windows, pinched at the top. Surreal, crumbling beauty. The shock of seeing something three-dimensional and real that had been seen before only as a flat image in a Bugs Bunny cartoon.

I wanted Venice to be a clean slate. On the *vaporetto*, I apologized to my father, and told him that I didn't mean what I had said. He did the same. We got off at the Gritti Palace. The staff whisked our bags away. The lobby was polished wood and fresh flowers, tapestried couches and blackamoor statue lamps.

It had been a long day, and upstairs we happily familiarized ourselves with the amenities of the huge cream-and-yellow room. The round mirror, the writing desk with its green velvet surface, the lights, the stationery, the glass chandelier. True Steinbergs, both, balmed by luxury.

We went in search of dinner. It was raining lightly, and the concierge at the Gritti handed us a big green umbrella as we hurried out the door. Classy. We first swept through the Piazza San Marco—the plaza is shaped like an upside down *L*. We entered through at the top of the long end, a stretch of identical colonnades, ending in the insanely ornate St. Mark's Basilica, where you turn right and see the Doges' Palace, the two pillars marking the entrance to Venice, and the Grand Canal beyond. It seemed both huge and in some way personal and intimate. No wonder Napoleon called it "the sitting room of Europe." Maybe going to a place you have heard of for a long time and actually seeing it always looks small, compared to the expanse of thought.

Dad marveled at how the *Empire State II* had anchored on his first cruise in the harbor, right there, framed between the two columns. That was the photo he had on his wall all those years—the *Empire State* in Venice. He squinted at the harbor as if he could see the ship before him.

Three little orchestras played for a handful of people. A few children danced energetically while the pigeons wheeled around in a great speckled mass.

After dinner we stopped by Harry's American Bar, an icon for those of us duped by the whole Hemingway/tough-guy/writer/drinker romantic lie. I hadn't realized the place would be so small, but I suppose that is fitting. Just a little room with a four-seat bar. We had a drink. Everyone else had the look of money about them—the cut of their suits, the knot of their ties, their easy manner. We perched tentatively on the two stools nearest the door, tourists in our functional jackets. Dad was distressed that the bar wasn't as he remembered it. He had seen Jerry Doyle through a window, and Doyle had gestured him in.

But there was no window. My father asked the bartender if the bar was at the original location. It was—you could see from the postcards it was the same from the 1930s. He asked a guy standing out front of the nearby Hanig's American Bar. He asked the front desk man of the Gritti. All vowed that Harry's was the same. My assurance that forty-five years was a long time, that maybe he misremembered it, maybe they replaced the window with a wall, meant nothing.

We plunged into the narrow streets behind the Gritti, in step for once, marveling at the narrow passageways, the snaking canals. My father pointed out that Venetians put their names on brass plaques next to their buzzers, as opposed to the slip of paper we use back home. "It's because they aren't going anywhere," he said, as a compliment to their permanence. It struck me, at that moment, that my father's observation about the plaques was more astute than anything that I, the big-shot journalist, had noticed on the entire trip.

I was energized to do more, about 10 P.M., but Dad said I would be surprised how tired I was. I managed to persuade him to go upstairs himself and get ready for bed while I had a nightcap at the Gritti bar. It was cozy, like a small, lush living room decorated in an explosion of colorful, headcheese marble. The Jack Daniel's cost $20, but I didn't care. The coasters were made of cloth, like little tablecloths. I took my drink and stepped onto the terrace, wet from the rain. The dome of the Basilica Santa Maria della Salute loomed, eerily, across the Grand Canal, lit up bright white against the black sky and water. It was incredible—a sight from *Little Nemo in Slumberland*. I broke into laughter. I had made it to Venice. I was here. Improbably, despite being mired in the middle-aged, middle-class grind of kids and work, bills and boredom, I had somehow crawled, momentarily, out of the deep rut I had shuffled for myself and found my way to Venice, dragging my father, of all people, along with me, to the Gritti Palace, where I was enjoying a drink on the terrace before heading up to my room. It was improbable but it was true. I was here, and nobody could take that away.

I laughed and laughed, out loud, unembarrassed.

My father and I had just one full day in Venice. We left the hotel, fresh and rested, the next morning at 7:35. My father announced that he wanted eggs. "I need protein," he said. I gingerly pointed out that eggs might be hard to find in Venice. We passed several places offering buffets—muffins, croissants, fruits, juices. I suggested a large, empty restaurant just off St. Mark's that offered a full spread for 18,000 lire. No eggs, but we could sit outside, with a view of the Grand Canal.

"I'm tired of toast," he said.

I was keenly aware of the delicacy, the peril of the situation, and gently explored one solution after another. We'd be having three meals and a big breakfast might not be a good idea. No go. I reminded him that he had said he wanted to lose weight. No. I tried what I thought was my trump: eggs are a typical *American* breakfast. He could have them all he liked, back in the United States.

Nothing worked. We had been walking nearly an hour, searching for eggs. I flashed on a morning-long quest for eggs. "How was Venice, Neil?" "Welllllll, I can tell you this: it doesn't hold a candle to Chicago, egg-wise!" I noticed some appealing sweets in the window of a little bakery shop where people were standing up, drinking coffee, and headed to the door.

"Do you mind if I eat something?" I said, hoping he'd see the sweets and be tempted and join me, forgetting whom I was dealing with. He said to go ahead. I joined a group of Italian workmen and ordered a splash of coffee with a hard sweet biscuit dribbled in chocolate.

I turned to tell Dad that he really should get something and be done with it—have his eggs in America—but he was gone. I felt a moment of fear that he had bolted, touched off by my sudden entry into the coffee shop. But then I saw him through the window, standing outside, his face set in a frown.

An elderly gent came in and ordered a port. The woman behind the counter poured Sandeman into an apéritif glass, which he held carefully to his lips. I watched him, and lifted my cup in a little salute, but he didn't notice me. The crowd was convivial and Italian. For the first time I felt like I had penetrated the tourist crust and was among actual locals. Real people. I wished very much that Dad was in there with me, leaning on the little bar, talking closely. Instead he stood out in the street, facing away, so I couldn't even gesture him in. I ate my dry biscuit quickly, washing it back with the strong coffee. How can I handle this a different way? I didn't want to be dismissive about his eggs.

Finishing, I walked out of the bar, rubbing my hands together, smiling largely. Respect, respect. "The Gritti Palace will have eggs," I said, wincing at thought of the cost. My father heartily agreed. I was going to draw attention to the probable expense, then thought of the chilling rejoinder he could easily make: "That wasn't an issue when it came to paying for your whiskey last night." I kept my mouth shut.

We were seated on a lovely patio facing the Basilica. He ordered eggs and asked for a basket of rolls. I stuck to coffee, squirming in my chair, aware of what was coming. At the next table a CEO type— obviously wealthy, his crisp shirt open at the neck, begging for a tie—kept waving cute small birds off his table, annoyed, as if they were vermin.

Finally, his eggs arrived, on a blue plate with a china dome cover. Set before my father, the dome was whisked away—ta-da!—to reveal a disgusting puddle of yellow glop. My father took a reluctant bite or two, then had the plate removed. We moved on, me sucking my front teeth, frantically trying to club the incident down into the hole in my brain.

Back at St. Mark's, I wanted to go up the tower of the Campanile and look around at the city, but we ran into a tout for Murano Island, the glass-making center. Where were we staying? he asked. The Gritti Palace. His eyes lit up. We would get a free water taxi trip to the island.

We were helped aboard a lovely wooden speedboat. I expected others to be funneled aboard, but as soon as we were settled it roared away, cutting through Venice and across the channel, marked by rough wooden posts that act to delineate lines of traffic. It was great to be on the water, sparkling in the morning sun.

The factory tour consisted of a cursory glimpse of two men blowing glass, and a two-minute lecture, before we were ushered into a gigantic store, filled with fabulously expensive stuff, the kind of glasswork the wives of the owners of big auto dealerships buy to fill their custom laminate breakfronts in Oak Brook. I admired the glassware—if I were in the market for a nice $250 set of six fancy champagne glasses I could have done well. But I wasn't.

The disappointed salesman ushered us faster and faster through progressively cheaper sections until we found ourselves out in front of the building. We had sat down on a bench, waiting for a boat to take us back, when we were shooed away, informed that we should go wait around the corner, through that gate. We walked through an automatic gate and it clicked shut and locked behind us. Trips back were for paying customers. We found ourselves in a weedy industrial area with no apparent way to go. But it was an island, as my father pointed out, so we started walking.

I was happy. Both of us were. Being ushered out the back gate and into this blank nowhere was a Chaplinesque touch. Surreal minor adversity is something both my father and I understand in our bones, and it always draws us closer together.

We picked our way across the island, stopping at other, less hard-sell factories. We caught a *vaporetto* back, and, two hours after we first stood before it that morning, were at the Campanile again, and got in the line—now huge—to get in.

"Do you want to wait in this line and climb the tower?" my father asked. "Yes," I snapped. "Yes, Dad, I do."

"Okay, I'll meet you back at the hotel at noon then," he said, and began to walk away. "Make it 1 P.M.," I called after him. "I'll meet you after lunch." After popping $35 for his pool of eggs, I figured, let him buy his own lunch.

There was a sweeping, panoramic view from the top of the tower. I wished my father were there with me to see it. A low cityscape of orange stone buildings, sliced up by canals and punctuated by towers. Bell towers. I looked up inside the tower I was in, at the array of giant bells, some so close you could reach up and touch them. I looked at my watch: 11:55. I examined the bells closely. They did not have the neglect of the centuries upon them. They were active, working, humongous bells right over our heads. I got in line for the elevator down. Minutes passed. I wondered how precise my watch was. I didn't get on the next ride down, but the one after. Stepping onto the street, I just had time to walk a few feet away and turn, to look back at the tower when noon was marked with an explosive bonging and peeling.

I can't imagine what it was like for the people up there.

We rendezvoused at 1 P.M. and headed out shopping, looking for something for the boys. Just when I was despairing at the lack of anything that couldn't be bought at the Toys 'R' Us on State Street in Chicago, I found a charming little store and bought a beautiful cutout paper theater, "Le Avventure di Pinocchio" and a pair of charming German lunchboxes. With my focus turning increasingly on going home, I missed the boys terribly and wanted to be sure I came home with an armful of presents, the way my father always had. His generosity abroad was legend in our family, my favorite story being the first time he went to Germany, about 1962. He had never before seen Steiff toys, those lovely mohair animals with the brass buttons in their ears, and bought so many that he had to buy another suitcase to carry them back. Then, when he got them home, he opened the suitcase before my sister and told her to pick out what she liked. She surveyed the gorgeous selection—a turtle, a lion, a lobster, an elephant, birds, and other assorted beasts—and burst out crying. "Didn't they have any *dollies?*" she wept. My poor father. Sometimes dads just can't win.

The last morning of the trip, Dad was up before 4 A.M. He woke me, intentionally. Get up, busy day. Our plane left at 2 P.M. He went to write in the bathroom. I went back to sleep and had a horrible nightmare about Grandpa Sam's funeral. It couldn't have been based on memory because I wasn't there. But his death was such a crossroads for my father's family, a shattering event, that it stands out in my mind as if I were a witness.

I woke up shaken. Dad was excited—he realized there was a Leonardo da Vinci exhibit, and we had time to hit it before checking out and leaving for the airport. The excitement spilled over into everything. He strode about the room, praising the pillows, the towels—"Most hotel towels are tiny," he said.

He praised the bath—it was heaven, paradise. "That's what civilization is all about," he said. I must take a bath. I did, I said, last night. "Take another," he said. "You can face anything after a bath like that." I took a shower. I wanted to see St. Mark's Place one last time. He wouldn't go with me; apparently the bath hadn't quite fortified him for *anything*. He wanted to stay at the room, standing by, ready to leave in three hours. So I went myself. I felt bad about it. Stopped at the same place as the morning before for another solitary chocolate biscuit, then took a slow stroll around the nearly empty St. Mark's, stopping to watch a two-year-old girl chase pigeons.

We headed to the Accademia for the Leonardo show. Dad was thrilled, extoling the mastery of Leonardo's drawings. I read the commentary cards and noticed that most weren't actually done by Leonardo, but by contemporaries. Dad was so happy, though, I kept it to myself. Da Vinci's famous drawing of a spread-eagle man within a square and circle was there, and I examined it closely. Always a small pleasure to check off one of the masterpieces on the list—not because anybody would be impressed, but just for the small bubble of pleasure that pops up every time you see it in a math book or a poster and think, with a belch of Burgermeister pride, *Yup, saw that.*

We got back to the room at 10:30 A.M., and I bolted back out. I didn't feel I had enough gifts for the boys—I had some, but I wanted a pile. I finally settled on a pair of colorful masks—a cat for Kent and a Pinocchio with a long, long nose for Ross.

Time to leave. There is a private dock at the Gritti, and we waited in the ornate, flower-filled lobby, our baggage around us. The water shuttle arrived. It was a small enclosed boat, all polished wood, with two long white cushioned benches facing each other. I sat in the bow, twisting to look through the open forward-facing window, practically bouncing in my seat, taking in Venice as it unfolded one last time in the fierce mid-June sun. Just as I was reflecting that I hadn't met any Italians, as I might have done without Dad in tow, a pair of men, naked to the waist, vigorously poling a tiny blue skiff through the chop, crossed our path. That would have to do.

My father sat on the opposite bench at the back of the cabin, with passengers between us, and as I scanned the scenery, I secretly studied him. The Old Commander, drawn and gray, protectively holding onto the handles of the shopping bags with gifts for my boys in them, even though we were on a small boat. He looked dignified, a king in exile, wearing practical traveling clothes, yet somehow still draped in lost majesty, shoulders squared, a remnant of faded pomp, of all the gilt-framed family portraits and double-headed eagles stuffed into his small exile's quarters. His hands were thin, roped with veins, clutching the bags. He looked old in the bright light of the canal. As much as I wanted to gaze at the Piazza San Marco as it disappeared, my eyes kept sweeping back to him as he, too, watched Venice recede. Our time was running out. It had run out. We had spent our day in Venice together, and now we were leaving and never coming back.

The airport in Venice was crowded and chaotic. It took us an hour to get to the front of the baggage check line. We were supposed to travel through Frankfurt, but flights were delayed—the Lufthansa clerk noted that we would miss our connection. She instantly solved the problem by rerouting us through London, via Alitalia, to connect at Gatwick Airport to an American Airlines flight from London to Chicago.

I was relieved to be on the plane, happy enough to tease my father. I pointed out we were seated in line with the engines. If one threw a fan blade, it could cut through the cabin and kill us. He didn't appreciate the joke. At Gatwick, we had forty-five minutes between flights. I was relaxed, eager to stop by a newsstand to pick up English newspapers to read on the flight over. My father wouldn't stop, but raced through the causeway. I trotted after him, chiding. He was still doing it, still rushing. What was the hurry? We had all the time in the world.

I was wrong. We didn't have all the time in the world. The clerk at the American Airlines counter stared at the Lufthansa ticket envelope as if I had handed her a piece of Monopoly money. "These are Lufthansa tickets," she said. "I can't honor them."

No, no, I said, smiling, confident, fully the man in charge. It's all in the computer. She tapped at her keyboard. It wasn't in the computer. The clerk in Venice had simply made us reservations. She had failed to actually book the flight, to issue whatever intra-airline chit was needed. My confidence drained out of my body and collected, like a damp puddle, in my shoes. The London clerk was indifferent. No, she could not summon a superior. No, she could not phone Lufthansa. They didn't even have a Gatwick office. Why don't you, she suggested, take a cab to Heathrow and work it out there?

Plunging into rush-hour London traffic—it was 4:30 P.M. locally—seemed a bad idea. My father was ready to crawl over the counter and throttle the clerk. I wanted to go home, fiercely. The line shifted uneasily behind us. Finally, with no other avenue open, I slapped my American Express card on the counter and bought two one-way tickets to Chicago on the spot for a thousand pounds.

We grabbed our luggage and bolted for the gate, running together flat out, frantic, only to skid to a halt behind a large Arab family being methodically examined by security. Finally we cleared the checkpoint, like a pair of divers, lungs bursting, breaking the surface. We raced for the plane and just made the flight, settling in our seats five minutes before they sealed the doors.

The plane took off. Now it was my turn to stew, to fixate. A thousand pounds is more than $1,500. I couldn't imagine Lufthansa coughing it up, not easily. The injustice rankled me. All we had done was follow their directions. I flipped open my laptop and composed what I was certain was only the first of many letters of protest and grievance and entreaty. "Lufthansa passengers holding valid tickets, following the instructions of Lufthansa personnel, should not be directed to distant cities and left to fend for themselves." I wrote.

My father was soothing. "Don't worry about it," he said. "Don't let it ruin your homecoming."

I tried. But even writing a letter didn't get it out of my system. I kept practicing my opening speech in court. Kept imagining the various steps needed to extract my money from the company, and the prospect of an extended, annoying, Javert-like quest hung over my head. I tried not to think about it. I told myself that if it was even lurking offstage, in the wings of thought, when I kissed my boys, that it would be my fault. A problem such as this is an invitation to be a better person: do not let anxiety infect your mind, but drive it out and take control of your consciousness, and think what you want to think. I knew this would be settled, though it might take some hounding, and that I would go through the necessary steps along with all the other dreary obligations that daily present themselves.

Sitting on the plane, I would work through all this, then immediately begin to worry, catch myself, and try to bat the thought away, actually picturing it as a baseball I would toss up and smash into the distance, or burn it up, pushing the thought away in a flash of flame. Dad was understanding, calm, comforting.

"This will be taken care of," he said. "I am absolutely certain of it."

I realized, to my chagrin, that my father was being far more sympathetic about my fixations than I had been about his. When he was worrying about meeting Mom in Charleston, about crime in Barbados or the dock in Naples, I had wielded my cold reason like a razor. Easy to dismiss the concerns of someone else as delusions, as phobias. But when those concerns are your own, they are not so easy to laugh at.

He put on his Bettie Page blackout mask and earplugs and wrapped himself in an airline blanket and slept for most of the flight. Poor tired guy, I thought, gazing at him, poor old tired guy. I felt a burst of pity. I had been too hard on him, the whole trip. And I hadn't even realized it. Problems that I thought were caused by his oddities were actually caused, or at least worsened, by mine. It wasn't that we were so distant, so different, that caused our conflicts. But that we were so close, so similar. I knew that—I had known that—but then forgot. In the rush and anxiety of the trip, in the challenge of being in a new place, first a ship, then a foreign country, I had lost sight of what I was doing. Lost sight of the important things.

The plane landed in Chicago. We claimed our bags. Before leaving the airport we stopped by the Lufthansa desk and filed our complaint. They were very understanding. I had booked my father into the O'Hare Hilton for the night—his flight for Denver was leaving the next morning. Before the trip, I had condemned him, in my mind, for having no interest in staying a day or two in Chicago, in seeing the boys while he was here. Now, after six weeks with him and nearly a day of air travel, I celebrated, privately, the wisdom of that choice.

He wanted to put me in a cab. I hadn't slept on the flight, brooding over the coming battle with the airline, and was rumpled and exhausted. But I felt responsible to check him in, to see him the last few steps. The hotel had the reservation. I walked him to the elevator. There was nothing for us to do now but part. Business people strode briskly by. The big faux potted plants observed us indifferently. Somewhere in the tepid oatmeal of my brain, the faint spark of a thought: this was the last obvious dramatic high point of the trip, and it, too, was passing by with a dull thud. Nobody made a speech.

"Thanks, Dad," I said.

"Sure," he said.

We hugged, awkwardly, and he disappeared into the elevator. The concierge said she'd call a cab, but none came. I ended up walking back to the airport to get one, like a dazed survivor shuffling out of the jungle. This is the last mile, I thought, the last test of my drained reserves and blown-out senses, to see if I can hold on until I reach my own safe port.

Night in Chicago. The cab hummed down the Kennedy Expressway, exited at California, swung east on Diversey. The familiar hot-dog stands, hardware stores, and apartment buildings, lit in the brown-orange sodium vapor streetlamps. Traffic congealed as we reached my crowded neighborhood near the lake. A left on Cambridge, a right on Surf, a left on Pine Grove, and we were there. I paid and dragged my stuff into the alcove. Just after 9 P.M.—way past the boys' bedtime. But I heard Ross's excited voice on the stairs as he rushed down to greet me—his mom had let him stay up late. They had been watching together from the upstairs window, waiting for me to come home.

I had worried that he would grow up in my absence, but he looked small, shockingly so. My tiny marionette son, my own Pinocchio, flapped his arms down the stairs, rushing down to greet me. Our place was immaculate—Edie must have been busy—and there was a banner, letters colored in crayon by the boys, a simple, splendid, WELCOME HOME DAD!!! I dumped my stuff on the living room floor, hugged Ross, kissed my wife, and was indeed, at last, home.

One Year Later

Lufthansa coughed up the money easily. I set my one souvenir of the trip, a green ashtray from Harry's Bar, on my desk and went on with life. My father actually did send me a bill for his cab ride to the airport in Denver, but I ignored it. The voyage began to recede into memory.

In the fall, my father took my mother to Italy. To my surprise, he insisted she see all the places we had gone, down to the same restaurants and hotel lobbies. Our trip had become a point of pride for him. "It's all he talks about," my mother said.

This astounded and puzzled me. He had complained the whole time on the trip. He was unhappy. He was counting the days. On the ship, it was a sacrifice. A favor to me. Now it was his great moment. I didn't understand.

The whole experience left me unsettled, particularly when it came to my boys. Suddenly the difference between what I was doing and what he had done seemed very small—uncomfortably small. Moments with the kids frequently sparked back to moments with him.

The family would be heading somewhere. I would be rushing ahead in that frantic manner of mine, and suddenly realize that Edie and the boys were ten paces behind me, hurrying along in my wake. I'd think of Naples and come to a skidding stop until they caught up.

Or when the weekend crew at the newspaper butchered a story of mine, it at first maddened me—I had worked *hard* on that story. I got angry, raging through the house, slapping my open palm on the doorframe, yelling. The boys hid.

Then I stopped, hand slowly lowering, as if wilting. And remembered my puzzlement as a child at my father's frustration at NASA—his fretting over rifts and pink slips and the Machiavellian jostlings of his fellow federal technocrats. I always viewed those moments as examples of his being stymied, thwarted, afraid. There had never been a question in my mind. That was what those memories meant.

But what if I had misinterpreted them? What if those episodes—rare, aggregated over the years—were just high ideals and lofty standards clashing with the compromised funk of reality? The head-slapping agony of seeing your good work mangled. That's the rationale I bestow on myself. Why withhold it from him because I was too young to understand?

The times when I would get into a righteous snit over something—arguing with my wife, arms crossed, mad and vowing to *stay* mad, because I was *right*, goddammit—the image of my father's face after I slipped off to smoke a cigar would return to me, that awful scowl, and I would mellow and begin to slide toward reconciliation.

Then, wonder of wonders, it happened. The unexpected note of grace—the grace I had lunged at so desperately the entire trip and bobbled so consistently—popped up in the most unexpected way.

In early spring, my father phoned me at work. He had pulled the schedule of the 2000 cruise of the *Empire State* off the Internet. They were going to Portugal. The ship would end up July 4 in New York City, taking part in the Tall Ships festival.

Did I, he asked, *want to go back? Should we go again?* I let the question hang in the air. Amazing, my father, always amazing. He wanted to go back. Why had I not expected this? Why was I always surprised? He wanted to go back. I was speechless. My silence must have prompted him to an explanation.

"I probably didn't maximize my opportunities," he said, quietly. "It was, in retrospect, a wonderful thing."

I told him I'd get back to him and hung up the phone.

In the sentimental movies that people feel compelled to make and to watch, the moment of reconciliation is always accompanied by weeping and hugging and schmaltzy music. How to show it otherwise? But those two sentences meant the world to me. It was all I was going to get from him. It was enough.

We probably didn't maximize our opportunities. It was, in retrospect, a wonderful thing.

The amazement flared and then died down, and I saw it all so clearly. Your life spools out, an impossibly long thread, the dramatic highlights so often obscured by expectations, the wonderful things hidden by routine and difficulty and heartbreak. The years melt away, irretrievable, and the most arduous moments, in hindsight, turn golden. "In retrospect, a wonderful thing." Not out of nostalgia, but because they *were* wonderful, were golden, only we were too stupid, too busy, too hurt, too human to recognize the glow at the time.

When I look back at the entire experience, I remember most fondly not Venice, not Dr. Richardson, that oak of New England, or St. Peter's Basilica, or even the grand sweep of the blue ocean, but my father and I bolting through Gatwick Airport together at full trot, like two detectives in an obscure action series—*Awkward Men! The Streets of Stress*—two lost boys, racing to get ourselves home.

Who knew that would be the highlight? My father and I running through a windowless causeway, frantic, our luggage bouncing at our sides, united in purpose. Together. While it is going on, life can be so confusing, when it isn't also bothersome and dreary and dull. It's so easy to complain, to fixate on the discomfort, on the mundane details of who is wrong and who is right and who said what to whom when, on how long the pier is and what the tickets cost, that you miss the tragic fact that your time is limited. That you are passing through the only life you will ever have, a life you will never return to, no matter how much you might want to later on. You can't go back and do it again. This is our time, the time we will miss so much when it is gone.

ACKNOWLEDGMENTS

S usan Raihofer struck the spark for this book one day over lunch in New York City. She then fanned the flame, encouraging and supporting me at every step, generously providing an endless amount of keen professional insight and effort, as well as cherished real friendship.

I also owe deep appreciation to her mentor and colleague, my agent for a decade, David Black, who shows unwavering faith in me.

Dan Smetanka, my editor at Ballantine, patiently waited for me to finish the manuscript, then crafted a fine edit and marshaled publishing might behind the book, which never would have been written without the cooperation of the State University of New York Maritime College, beginning with Stan Melasky and continuing through Admiral David C. Brown, Karen Markoe, and Captain Joseph Ahlstrom. Thanks to them, and to the officers and cadets of the Training Ship *Empire State VI*. I'll always be proud that I sailed aboard her. Special thanks to Richard Corson, the librarian at Fort Schuyler, and Dr. John Richardson.

Many people shared their reminiscences with me. Particular thanks to Jack and Sandy Goldberg, Sid Seidenstein, Herman Shapiro, Paul Parker, Bill Sembler, Jr. and Sr., Jim DeSimone, Brian McAllister, Chester Krug, Millie Steinberg, and Morty Steinberg.

At the *Sun-Times*, the demands this book placed on my time were dealt with sympathetically by Joyce Winnecke, the managing editor. Metro editor Don Hayner read part of the manuscript and provided extremely useful advice. Thanks as well to Rob Feder, Steve Huntley, and ace photographer Bob Davis, the soul of professionalism. And to the most colorful man I ever hope to work for, Nigel Wade—as Harold Ross used to say—"God bless and God damn."

A special thanks to Richard Roeper and Bill Zwecker, my constant friends. Alison True, at the *Chicago Reader*, has been a supportive and generous editor, as has Dick Babcock at *Chicago* magazine. Thanks as well to Rich Cohen, Mark Healy, Sheila Gibson, and to Mark Jacob at the *Chicago Tribune*, who gave the manuscript a close read.

Awe and gratitude go to Adam Gopnik, the *New Yorker*'s peerless star, for his wise insight and kind encouragement, saving me at my moment of extremity, like General LaSalle.

Bob Kurson was there for me during much of the struggle to write this book, and it was a wonderful thing to have him in my corner. "It is not often," E. B. White wrote, "that someone comes along who is a true friend and a good writer."

The decades roll by, but my dearest friends stand with me. I give a knowing wink to Rob Leighton and Cate Plys, who took the bus together up to the Bronx—the *Bronx*, for Chrissakes!—to wave goodbye to the ship, as well as to their spouses, Ron Garzotto and Val Green. Thanks to Jim and Laura Sayler and their lovely, smart girls, Claire and Elaine, as well as to Kier Strejcek and Cathleen Cregier. My father and I were given the proper send-off dinner by my hip Manhattan pals, Robert Ackerman and Carol Weston. Thanks as well to Di Thys—take those malaria pills!—Larry and Ilene Lubell, Don and Elisa Staniszewski, and Laura Vitez.

Acknowledgments

My in-laws, Irv and Dorothy Goldberg, are the best people I've ever met, and their tireless, cheerful efforts on behalf of myself and my family can never be repaid, nor can the value of their loving extended family—Jay and Janice Sackett, Alan and Cookie Goldberg, and all their girls, Julia, Esther, Rachel, Sarah and Beth—be overestimated. Not to forget Professor Don Goldberg, all the way over at Occidental College in California.

At last, thanks to my own family, who bear the brunt of my profession with general grace and good cheer. My brother, Sam, soldiers with me in Chicago through the daily claw and grind. My sister, Debbie, does the best she can. Words are insufficient to acknowledge my wife, Edie Steinberg, who was always enthusiastic about this project, despite the many burdens it placed on her. She also gave the draft a damn fine edit—though she'd strike out the word *damn*—and made me seem a better writer than I actually am.

Thanks as well to my boys, Ross and Kent, for being the joy of the world and for letting Daddy write. Finally, a heartfelt thanks to my mother, June Steinberg. This book is dedicated to you because you put up with the both of us and because you talked him into going, twice.

And a formal thank-you, though it seems inadequate at the end of project like this, to my father, Robert Steinberg, who had doubts—enormous doubts, huge doubts, like Macy's Thanksgiving Day Parade balloons—but went along anyway, enduring my company and the rigors of the sea. Thanks, Dad. I love you.